Have lots of fun darling 1991
all my love as a

TWILLEYS CONVERSION CHART FOR U
ONDORI HANDICRAFT TITLES

YARN	RECOMMENDED YARN	HOOK SIZES RECOMMENDED		
D.M.C.				
No. 3	Twilleys Southern Comfort	1.50	1.75	2.00
No. 4	Twilleys Lyscordet	2.00	2.50	3.00
No. 5	Twilleys Southern Comfort	1.50	1.75	2.00
No. 15	Twilleys Twenty	1.00	1.25	1.50
No. 18	Twilleys Twenty	1.00	1.25	1.50
No. 20	Twilleys Twenty	1.00	1.25	1.50
No. 30	Twilleys Twenty	1.00	1.25	1.50
No. 40	Twilleys Forty	0.60	0.75	1.00
Soft Twisted	Twilleys Southern Comfort	1.50	1.75	2.00
Cotton Lustre C.B. (art 980)	Twilleys Lyscordet	2.00	2.50	3.00
Cordinnet Special (art 151)	Twilleys Twenty	1.00	1.25	1.50
ANCHOR MERCER-COTTON				
No. 5	Twilleys Southern Comfort	1.50	1.75	2.00
No. 8	Twilleys Southern Comfort	1.50	1.75	2.00
No. 10	Twilleys Twenty	1.00	1.25	1.50
No. 30	Twilleys Twenty	1.00	1.25	1.50
No. 40	Twilleys Forty	0.60	0.75	1.00
Fashion Tone	Twilleys Southern Comfort	1.50	1.75	2.00
MERCERIZED CROCHET COTTON				
No. 3	Twilleys Southern Comfort	1.50	1.75	2.00
No. 4 Soft Twist	Twilleys Southern Comfort	1.50	1.75	2.00
No. 18	Twilleys Southern Comfort	1.50	1.75	2.00
No. 20	Twilleys Twenty	1.00	1.25	1.50
No. 30	Twilleys Twenty	1.00	1.25	1.50
No. 40	Twilleys Forty	0.60	0.75	1.00
No. 50	Twilleys Forty	0.60	0.75	1.00
No. 60	Twilleys Forty	0.60	0.75	1.00
No. 70	Twilleys Forty	0.60	0.75	1.00
QUICK CROCHET COTTON				
Soft Twist	Twilleys Southern Comfort	1.50	1.75	2.00
Olympus Amy Granda	Twilleys Forty	0.60	0.75	1.00

Twilleys Lystra Stranded Embroidery Cotton can be used instead of D.M.C. or Anchor embroidery floss

ONDORI HANDICRAFT TITLES AVAILABLE FROM TWILLEYS OF STAMFORD
ROMAN MILL, STAMFORD, LINCS. PE9 1BG TEL: 0780 52661

★Published by ONDORISHA PUBLISHERS, LTD.,
32 Nishigoken-cho, Shinjuku-ku, Tokyo 162, Japan.
★Sole Overseas Distributor : Japan Publications Trading Co., Ltd.,
P.O.Box 5030 Tokyo International, Tokyo, Japan.
★Distributed in the United States by Kodansha International/USA Ltd.,
throgh Harper & Row, Publishers, Inc., 10 East 53rd Street, New York, New York 10022.
Australia by Bookwise ; 1 Jeanes Street, Beverley, South Australia 5007, Australia.

10 9 8 7 6 5 4 3 2

ISBN 0-87040-754-6
Printed in Japan

Floral Designs

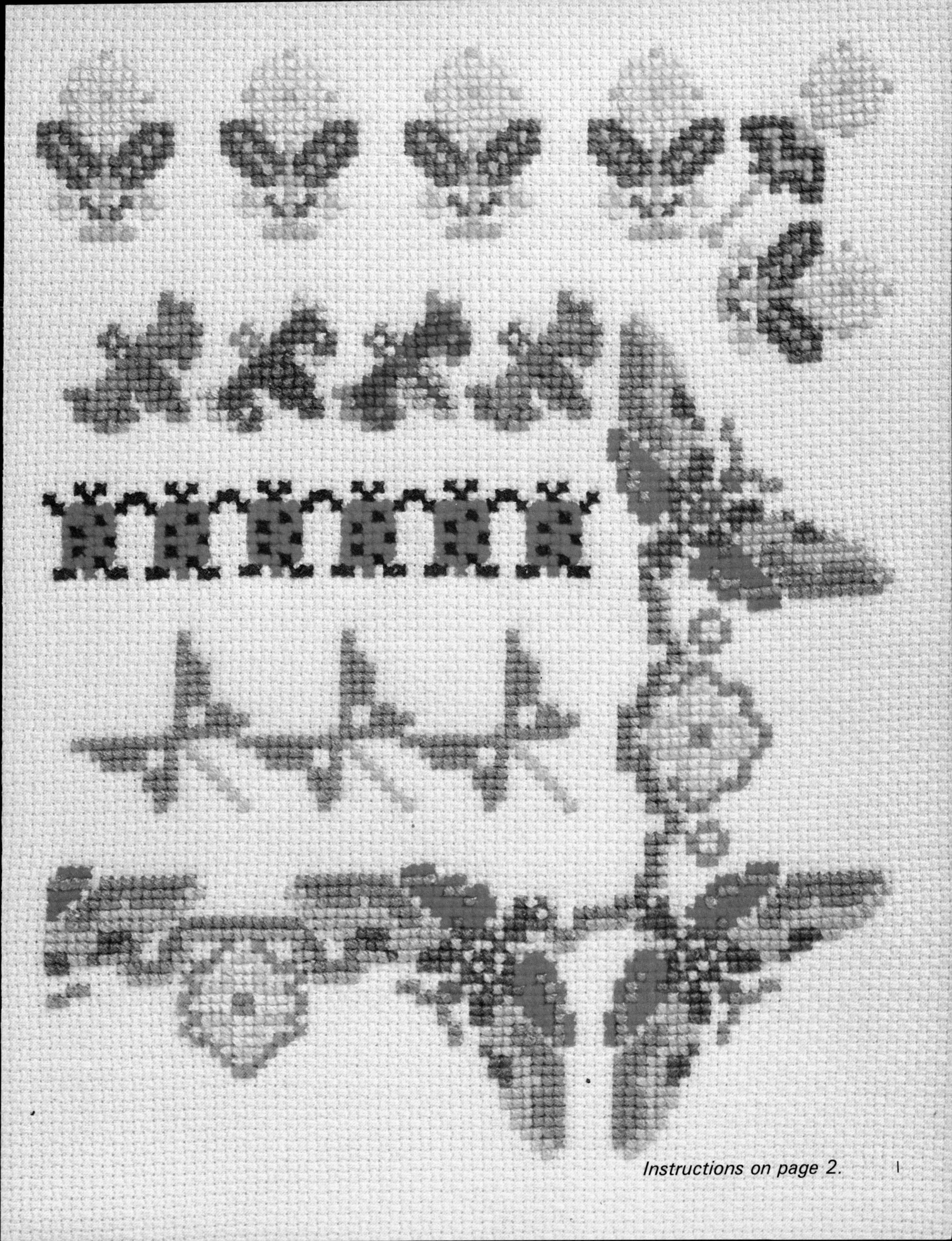

Instructions on page 2.

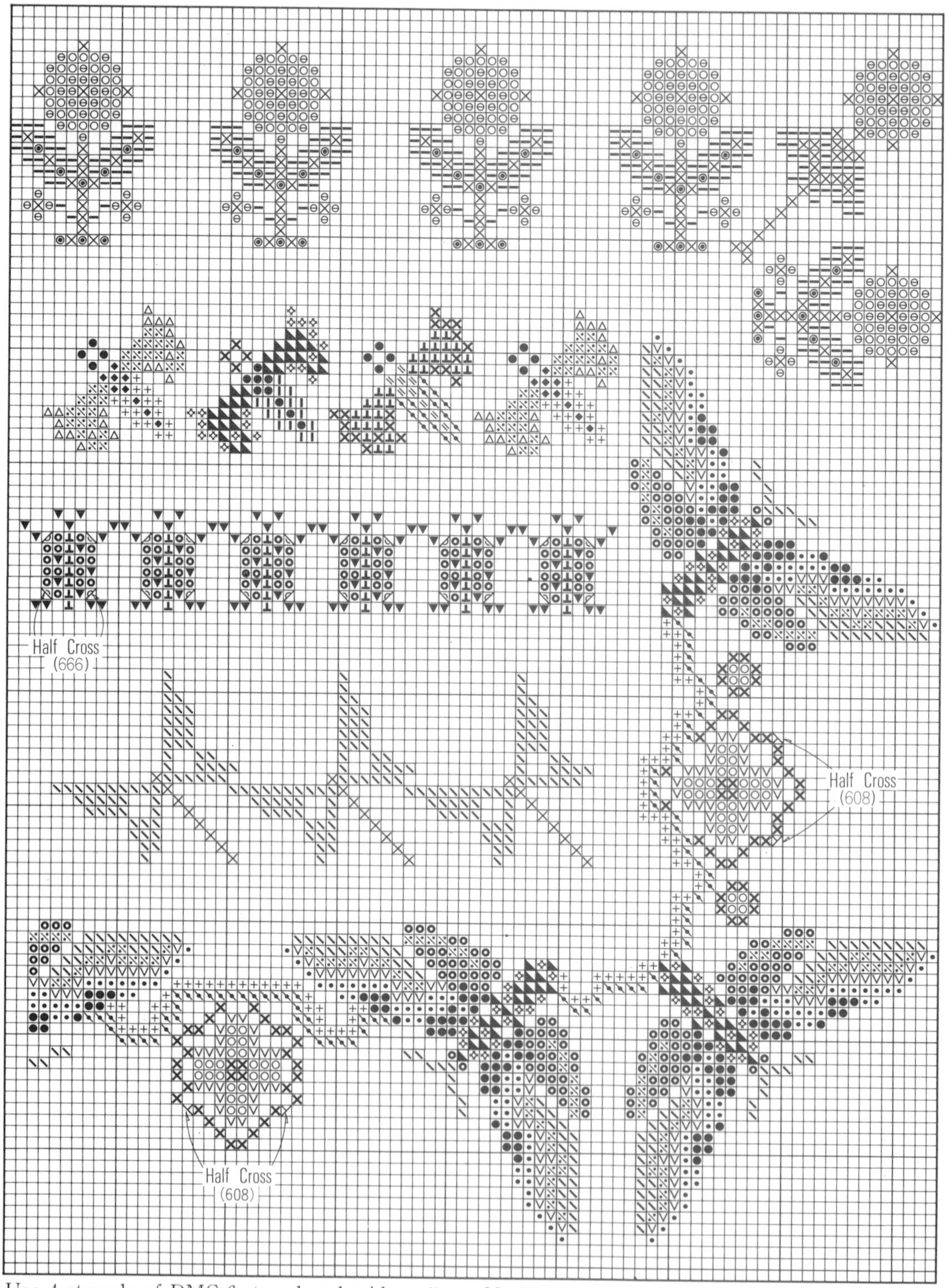

Use 4 strands of DMC 6-strand embroidery floss, No.25.

【Reds】 ⧅=606 ☒=608 ⊥=816 ◙=666 ⊡=957 【Yellows】 ◉=740 ⊠=741 ⊖=726 ○=727 Ⅴ=725

【Browns】 ●=433 ◣=400 【Violets】 △=718 ◆=917 ⧄=553 【Greens】 ▬=701 ▮=909 ⊞=912

⟐=472 ⧄=954 【Blue】 ⁘=996 【Black】 ▼=310

Shown on page 112.

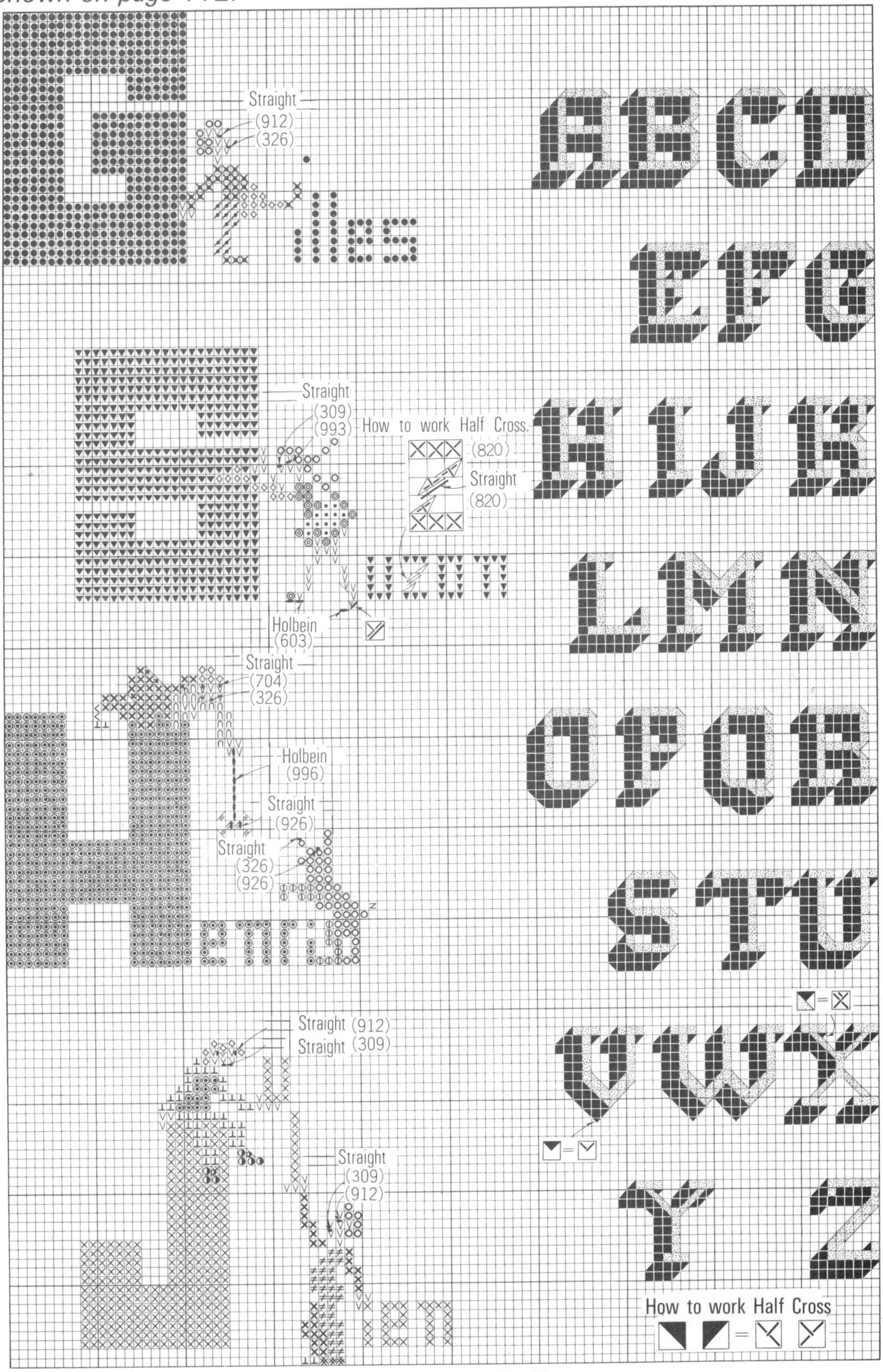

Use 3 strands of DMC 6-strand embroidery floss, No.25.

【Reds】 ■=817 ⁘=3689 ●=326 ⧄=946 ◎=603 //=776 【Yellows】 ◇=971 【Browns】 ○=841 V=951 Φ=976 Z=434 【Violet】 •=554 【Greens】 ☒=471 ◉=704 <=368 ⊥=701 ⋇=912 【Blues】 ▼=820 ∩=827 ☒=996 ☒=598 ◑=517 ≠=813

 Instructions on page 6.

Instructions on page 7.

Use 4 strands of DMC 6-strand embroidery floss, No.25.

【Reds】 ● = 326 • = 776 ⌋ = 899 ⊥ = 606 ◒ = 900 【Yellow】 ≠ = 973 【Browns】 ▲ = 400 ⊕ = 680

◉ = 783 ∩ = 822 ⧅ = 840 > = 3047 【Violets】 ◐ = 208 ◎ = 209 ▼ = 915 【Greens】 ◣ = 368 ☒ = 988

V = 704 Z = 906 ◣ = 319 ◇ = 954 【Blues】 ◣• = 797 ǁ = 825 ◇ = 827 【Black】 ■ = 310

Use 4 strands of DMC 6-strand embroidery floss, No.25.

【Reds】 ◣=815 ◎=900 ▼=3685 △=3688 •=3689 ■=666 ⊥=601 【Yellows】 ○=353 ∩=741 ❖=742 ⟍=971 【Browns】 ▥=400 +=613 【Violets】 ⦿=208 V=211 ◎=209 【Blue】 ◆=797 【Greens】 ●=937 ◐=3347 ✕=3348 ⊠=700 ⊕=704 ⟍=905

 Instructions on page 10.

Instructions on page 11.

Use 5 strands (Top)・4 strands(Bottom) of DMC 6-strand embroidery floss, No.25 unless otherwise indicated.

【Reds】 ◉=900 •=946 【Yellow】 +=741 【Greens】 V=369 ■=890 \=988 【Blue】 X=826

Use 5 strands of DMC 6-strand embroidery floss, No.25.

【Reds】 ● = 601 ☒ = 818 ◉ = 335 ▼ = 3685 • = 3688 【Yellows】 ▮ = 971 ◣ = 972 【Violets】 △ = 209
◐ = 550 ┴ = 552 【Greens】 ✕ = 699 ┘ = 905 ◥ = 907 【Blues】 ◘ = 517 V = 800 ‖ = 797 ✧ = 799 ○ = 807

 Instructions on page 14.

Instructions on page 15.

Use 4 strands of DMC 6-strand embroidery floss, No.25 unless otherwise indicated.

【Reds】 • = 304 ● = 902 Ф = 353 ┫ = 899 ▲ = 666 ◆ = 815 ⊕ = 947 【Yellows】 △ = 742 ⊖ = 727 ╳ = 971 【Browns】 ◐ = 435 ✧ = 976 ◘ = 433 ▼ = 400 ┻ = 801 【Violets】 ◇ = 209 ◣ = 550 ◉ = 915 【Greens】 ╲ = 469 Σ = 471 ∩ = 472 ■ = 890 ⋋ = 906 ⊠ = 911 ≠ = 3348 + = 907 ‖ = 909 > = 912 ❙ = 368 ╲ = 470 ✖ = 937 ◢ = 905 V = 369 ◎ = 954 【White】 ○

Use 4 strands of DMC 6-strand embroidery floss, No.25 unless otherwise indicated.

【Reds】 ☒=350 △=352 ⊙=309 •=666 ●=902 ◆=898 ◎=356 ⧵=434 ⊞=783 ◉=918 ▮=841 ▥=909 ∩=472 ✖=907 【Black】 ■=310

【Yellows】 ✧=742 ⦶=740 【Browns】 ○=613

【Greens】 ∨=471 ↘=733 ◐=319 ＞=704

 Instructions on page 18.

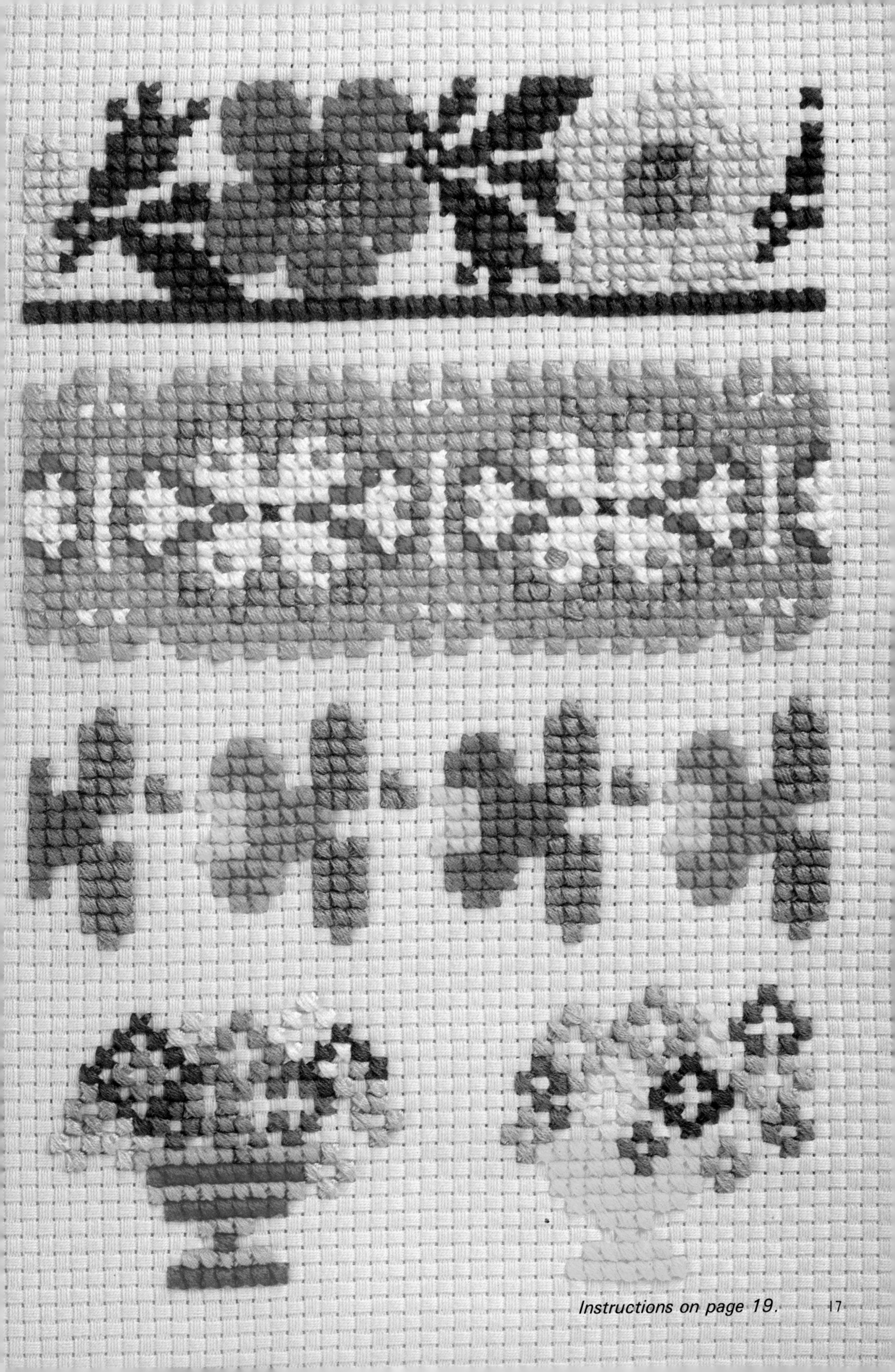

Instructions on page 19.

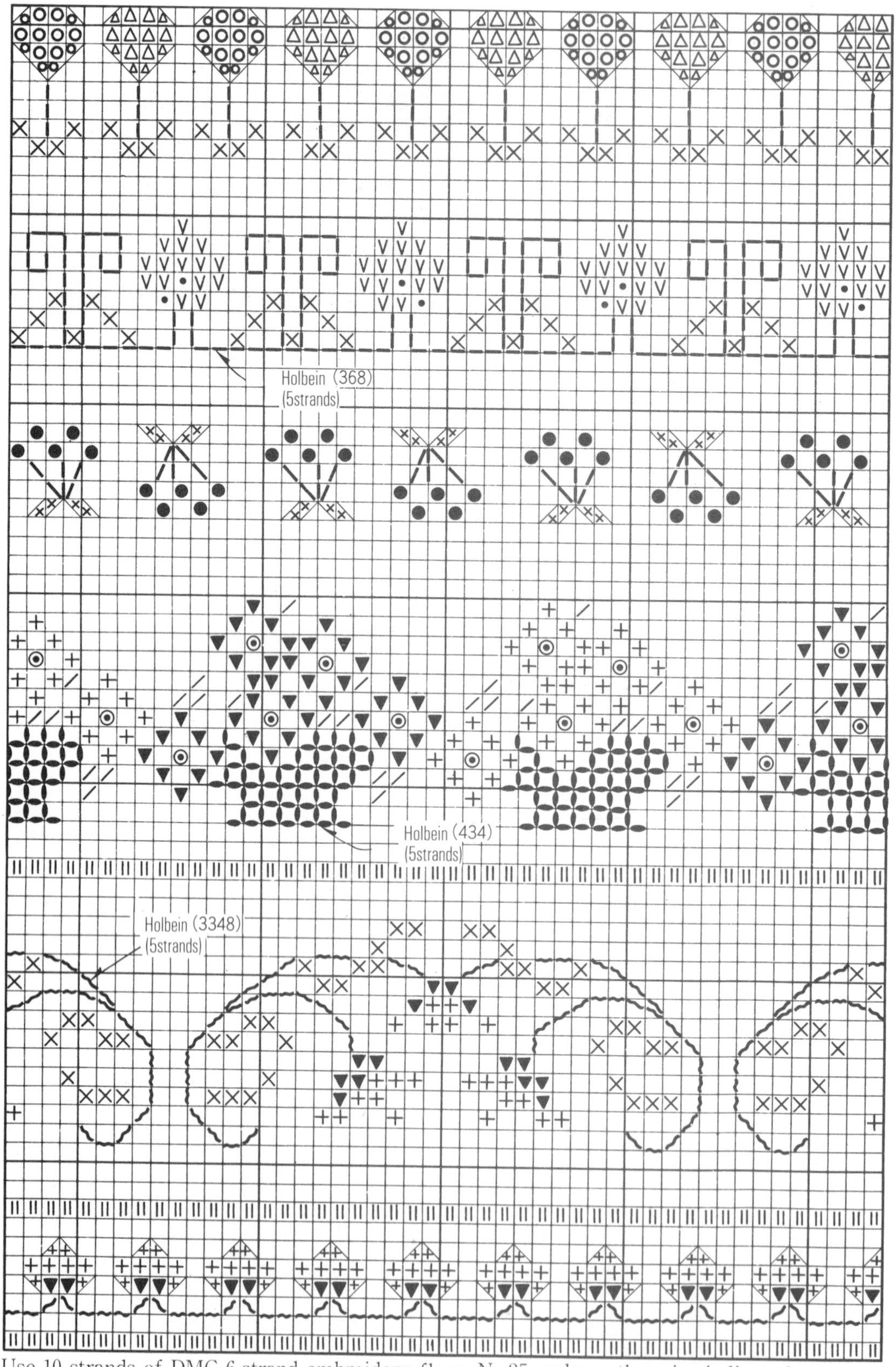

Use 10 strands of DMC 6-strand embroidery floss, No.25 unless otherwise indicated.

How to work Half Cross

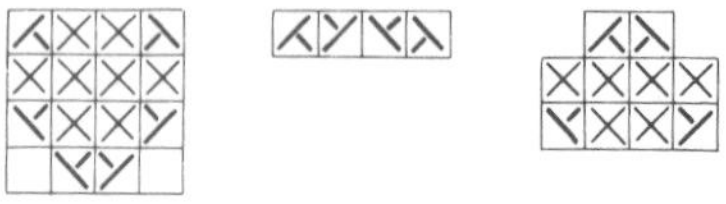

【Reds】 ● = 666 ▼ = 309 + = 3689 【Yellows】 △ = 725 ◉ = 444

【Brown】 O = 783 【Violets】 • = 208 V = 209 【Grey】 || = 3072

【Greens】 X = 368 / = 704

Use 10 strands of DMC 6-strand embroidery floss, No.25.

【Reds】 ◆=326 ☒=899 ▲=947 ‖=666 ◇=948 【Yellows】 [dotted slash symbol]=742 ☒=444 [hook symbol]=445 ◎=740

【Violets】 ■=550 ◎=552 ☒=3041 ✧=3042 ◢=209 ∩=211 ◣=553

【Greens】 ●=699 ◐=991 ◘=993 ⋋=906 [half-shaded circle]=701 ⑊=702 ＋=704 ▮=911 △=3348

【Blues】 ○=747 ▼=806 •=807 ⊕=519 ⊥=597 ≠=598 ⧺=800 【White】 V

Dreamland

Instructions on page 22.

Instructions on page 23.

Use 4 strands of DMC 6-strand embroidery floss, No.25.

【Reds】 ◥=606 ○=776 ◒=816 ●=666 •=601 Σ=604 【Yellows】 ⊙=725 ∩=727 ⟍=741

【Browns】 ◿=400 V=945 ▼=922 ‡=842 ▲=938 【Violets】 ◆=208 ⧺=211 ⊥=3041 ◇=554

【Greens】 ‖=702 ╳=704 ◐=699 ⧅=993 ⊕=906 ▮=991 ◣=701 ✖=703 【White】 +

【Blues】 ◉=996 ┫=518 ◎=519 △=747 ━=793 ✧=794 【Black】 ■=310

Use 4 strands of DMC 6-strand embroidery floss, No.25.

【Reds】 ◆=900 ☒=602 ●=666 ○=776 ◑=893 ⧖=963 【Yellows】 ◇=307 ◉=740 △=742 ▥=444 【Browns】 ▽=945 ▲=898 ◢=400 ⧗=436 【Violets】 ☒=554 ▼=718 ⊕=209 【Grey】 ⊣=415 【Greens】 ⧄=993 ◣=989 ✧=3348 ◐=699 •=702 ⊠=704 【Blues】 ⊞=800 ◎=519 ⋒=828 ⦿=996 【Black】 ■=310 Half Cross ◩ ◪ = 704 666

Instructions on page 26.

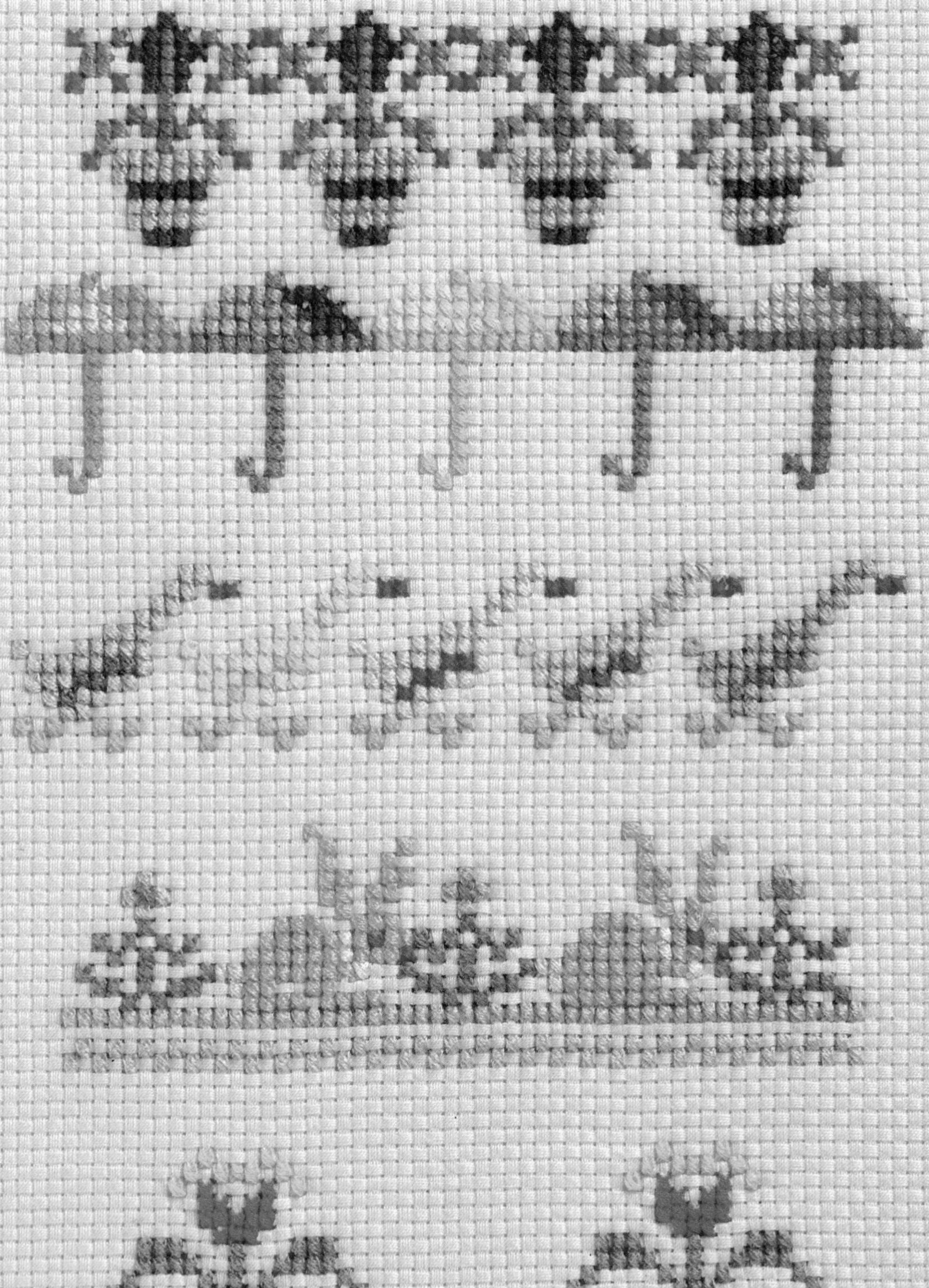

Instructions on page 27.

Use 5 strands of DMC 6-strand embroidery floss, No.25.

【Reds】 ☒=326 Ⓥ=776 ▼=309 ◆=600 ◐=602 △=3688 【Yellows】 ○=444 ◉=740 ☒=742 ◥=744 【Browns】 ●=433 ⊙=436 ⟐=842 ⊞=951 【Violet】 ⦶=209 【Greens】 ▮=912 ⊠=704 ▮▮=905 【Blues】 •=827 【Grey】 ┫=318

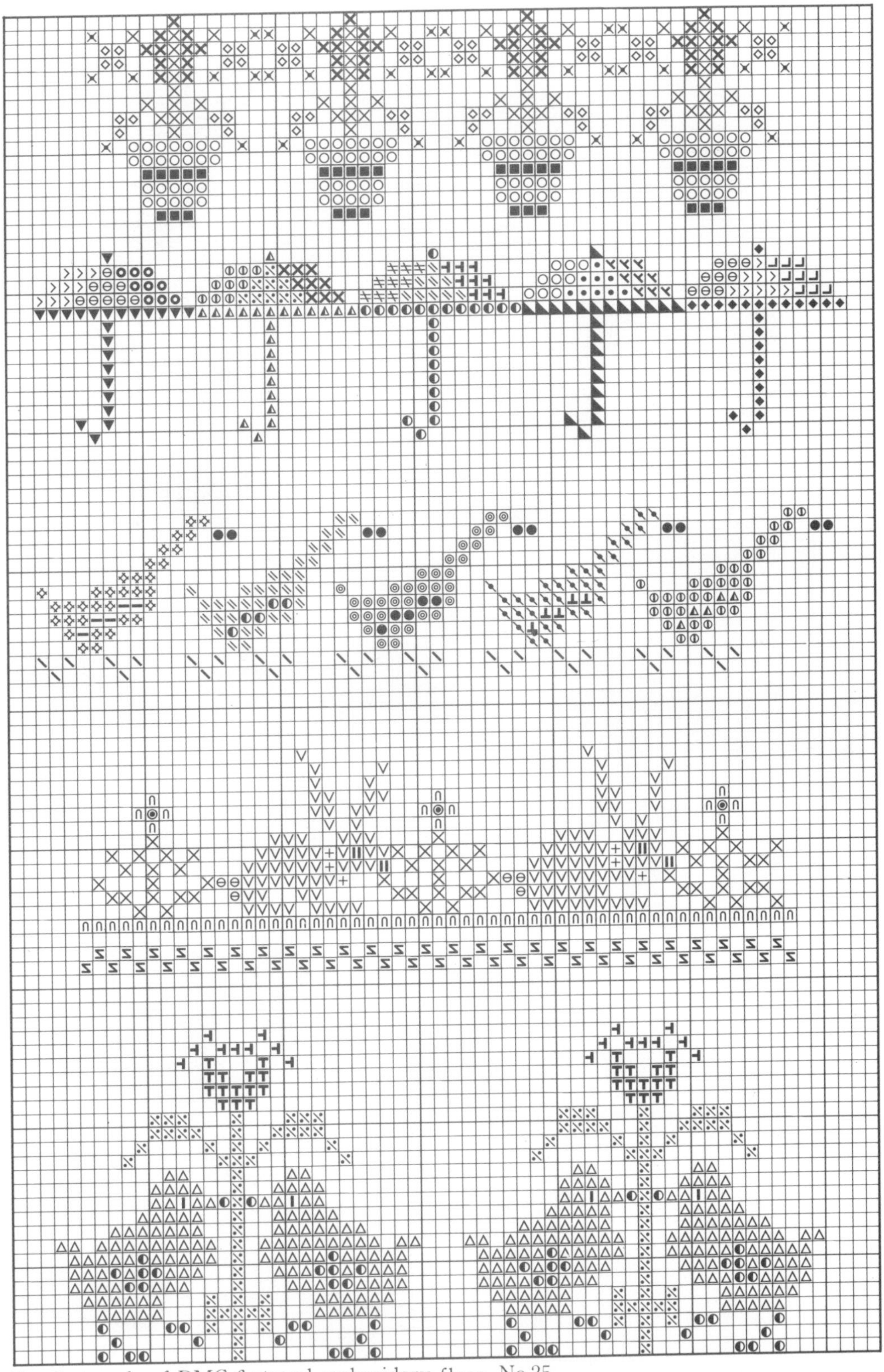

Use 5 strands of DMC 6-strand embroidery floss, No.25.

【Reds】 ⨯=666 >=604 ⊖=605 ▼=892 ◙=893 ●=606 ◎=776 ‖=350 I=601 T=602

【Yellows】 ≠=727 ◐=741 ┫=742 ▧=743 △=444 【Browns】 ▬=640 ⟡=644 ╲=783 V=402

+=739 【Violets】 ■=550 ⋖=552 •=209 ┘=718 ◆=917 ⊥ 208 ↘=211 ⊙=553 ∩=554

【Greens】 ✖=909 ⊠=912 ▲=702 ⁘=703 Φ=3348 【Blues】 ○=800 ◇=996 ◢=807 Σ=3325

 Instructions on page 30.

Instructions on page 31.

Use 6 strands of DMC 6-strand embroidery floss, No.25.

【Reds】 ● = 666 △ = 776 ◎ = 602 【Yellows】 ‖ = 444 + = 745 | = 727 V = 746 【Browns】 ＼ = 922 ◢ = 400 ▼ = 898 • = 840 【Violets】 ∩ = 209 【Greens】 ⋋ = 906 ◐ = 909 ✕ = 912 【Black】 ■ = 310 【Blues】 ◣ = 806 ◇ = 996

Use 6 strands of DMC 6-strand embroidery floss, No.25.

【Reds】 ●=817 ◙=3328 ○=760 △=899 【Yellows】 ◇=445 ⦶=725 ∩=744 【Violet】 ▼=550

【Browns】 ⊠=400 •=420 V=644 ⋋=822 ⊞=945 ◎=922 ◆=938 【Greens】 ‖=911 ┫=701

╲=503 【Blues】 ◐=791 ✖=597 ╳=598 ✧=800 【Black】 ■=310

 Instructions on page 34.

Instructions on page 35.

Use 4 strands of DMC 6-strand embroidery floss, No.25.

【Reds】, ◒=321 ┫=326 ◆=498 ⦶=603 ●=309 ▼=347 ◢=900 ⊕=3326 【Yellows】 ‖=742
△=743 【Browns】 ◉=355 ▮=436 ┘=840 ▽=945 ┻=922 【Violets】 ⋋=210 ⋌=209 •=718
【Greens】 ▷=703 ✖=911 ∩=913 ○=987 ╳=3347 【Blues】 ◥=794 ⧺=798 ◎=826 ⊖=519
【Greys】 ⊠=318 ⟐=415 【Black】 ■=310 【White】 +

Use 4 strands of DMC 6-strand embroidery floss, No.25.

【Reds】 ◒=321 【Yellows】 ▲=725 ⊘=726 △=743 ‖=742 ━=971 【Browns】 ⊥=922 V=945 T=434 【Violets】 Σ=553 •=718 【Greens】 O=987 ╳=3347 ✖=911 ∩=913 【White】 + 【Blues】 ⋠=813 ◎=826 ◇=794 【Greys】 ⊠=318 ⍀=647 【Black】 ■=310

Toyland

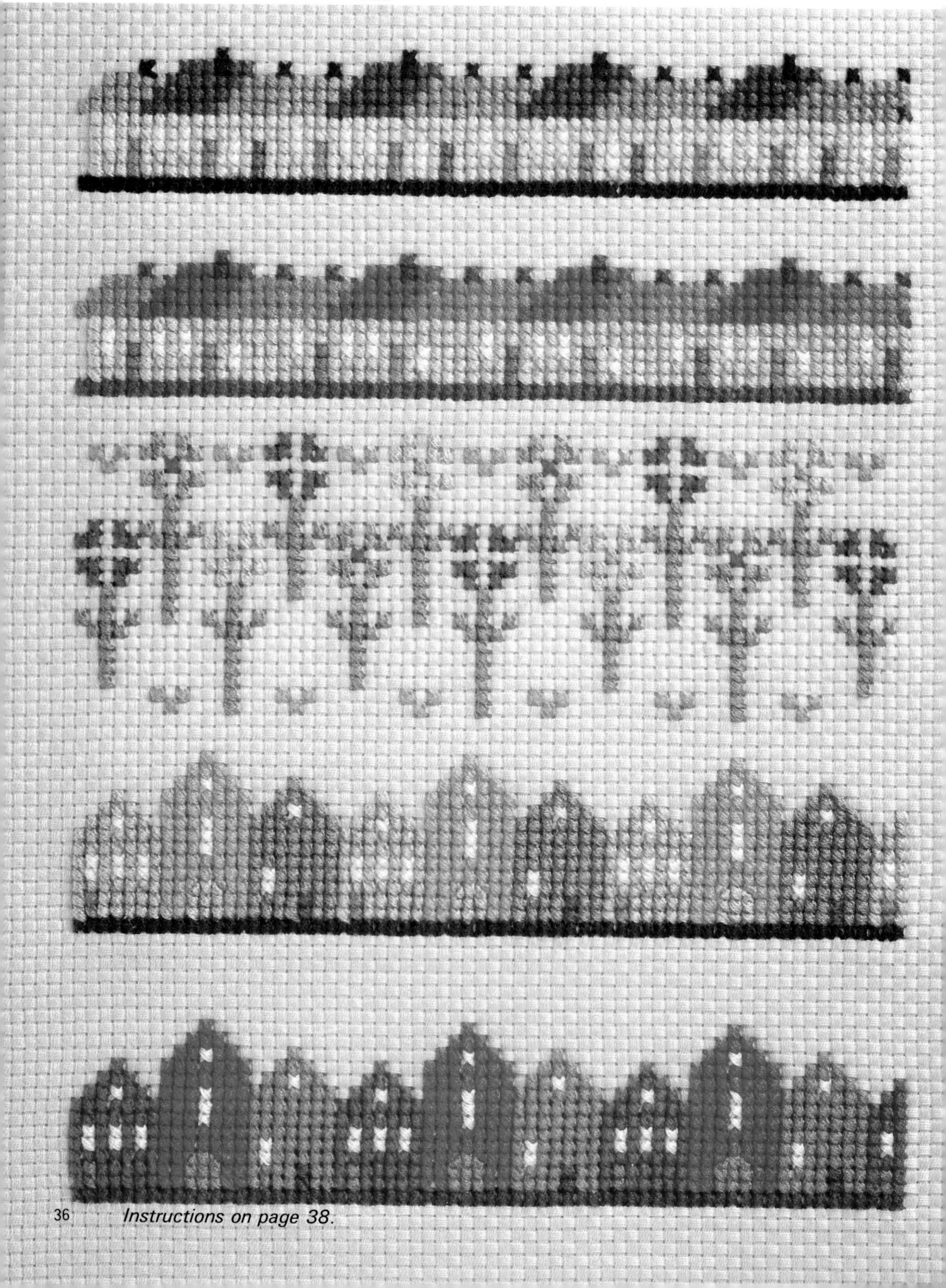

Instructions on page 38.

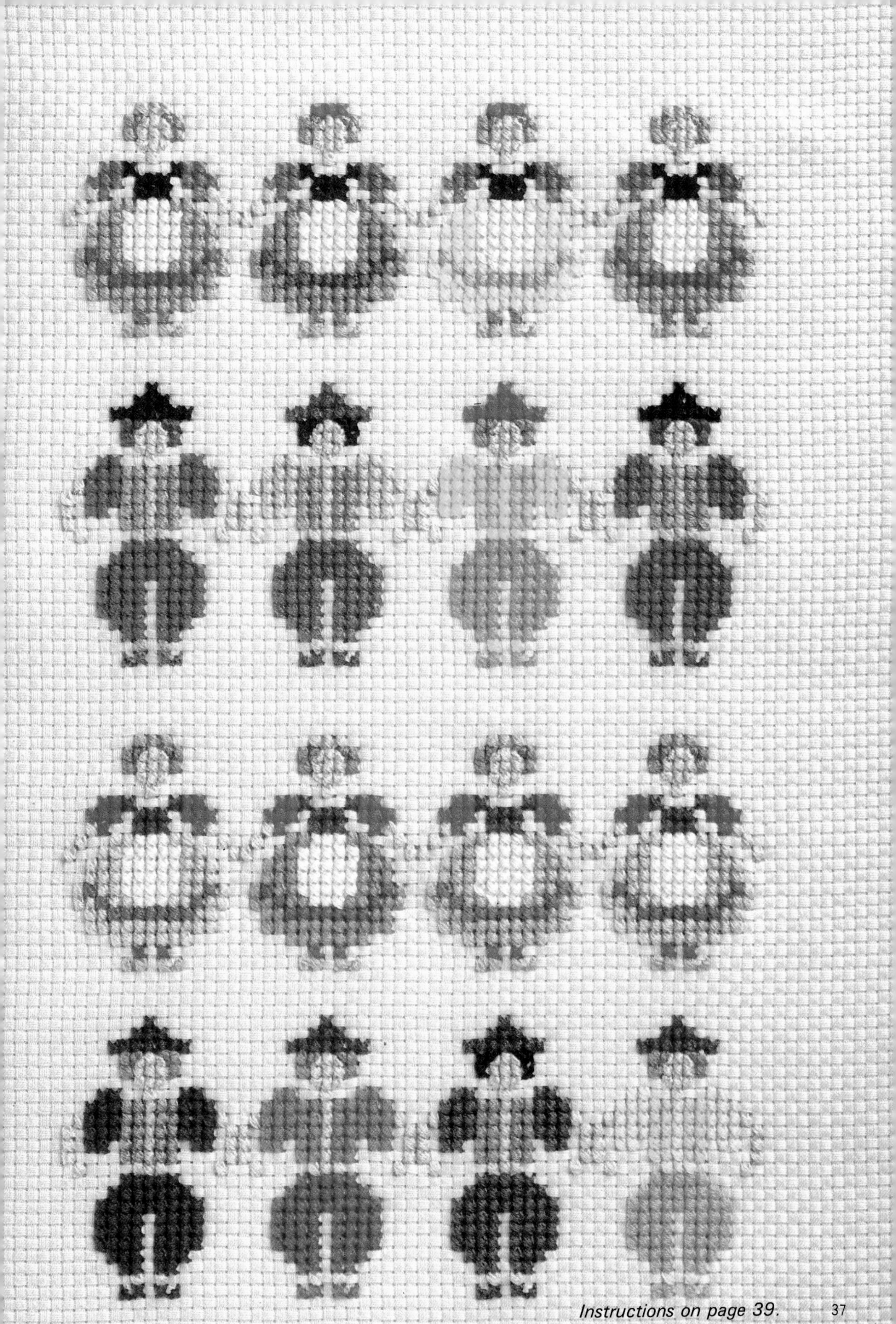

Instructions on page 39.

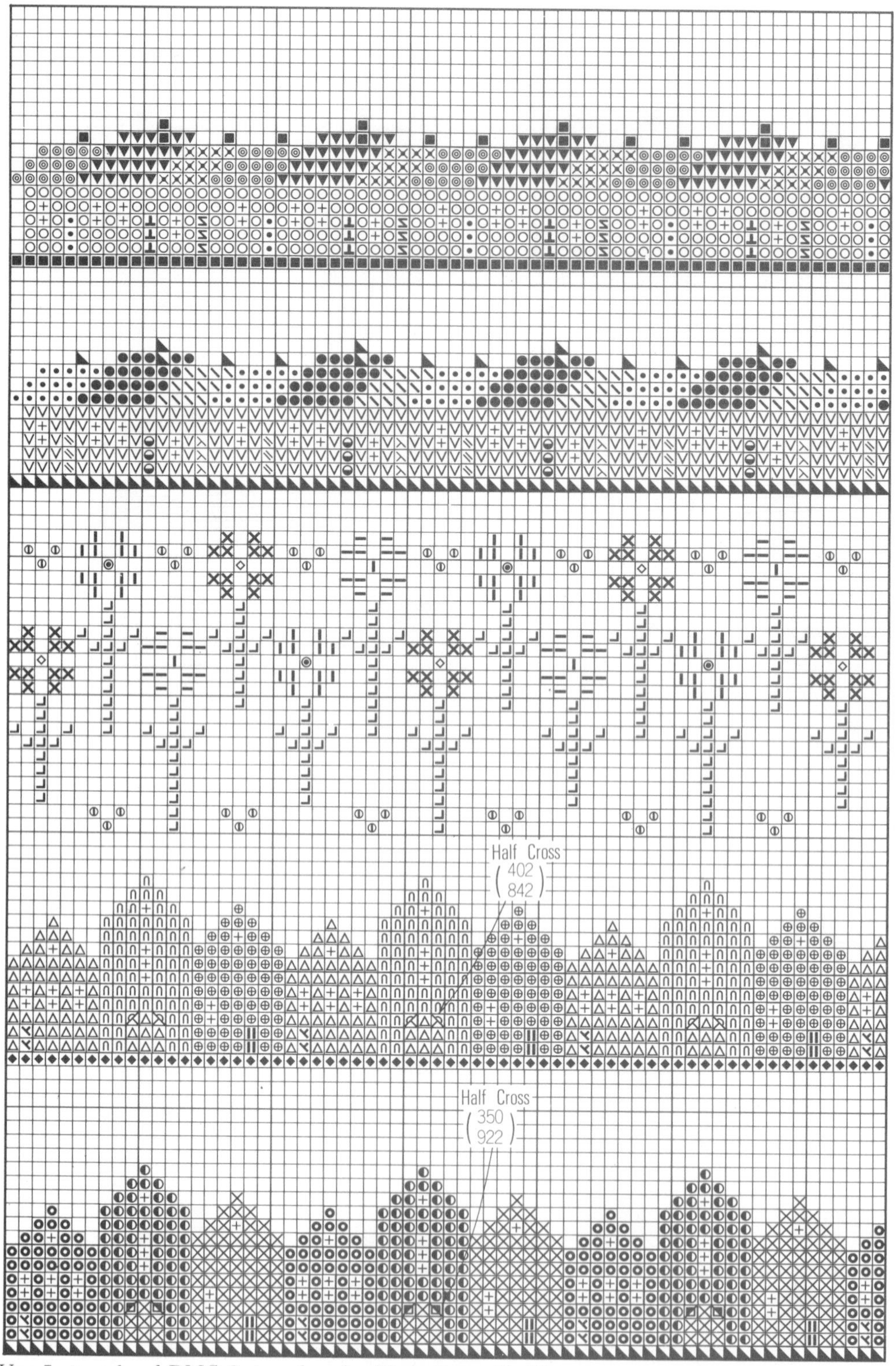

Use 5 strands of DMC 6-strand embroidery floss, No.25.

【Reds】 ● = 600 ╲ = 602 • = 603 V = 605 ◎ = 666 ◐ = 350 ⊙ = 900 【Yellows】 ⦶ = 740 ◇ = 445
【Browns】 ◣ = 300 ◒ = 680 ⋋ = 739 ◆ = 938 ⊕ = 841 △ = 842 ‖ = 433 ⋌ = 435 ∩ = 402 ☒ = 922
【Violet】 ❙ = 209 【Greens】 ▼ = 991 Z = 3346 ⅃ = 906 【Blues】 ⊥ = 518 ⊠ = 597 ◎ = 927
○ = 828 ⧅ = 322 ✕ = 517 ━ = 800 【Black】 ■ = 310 【White】 +

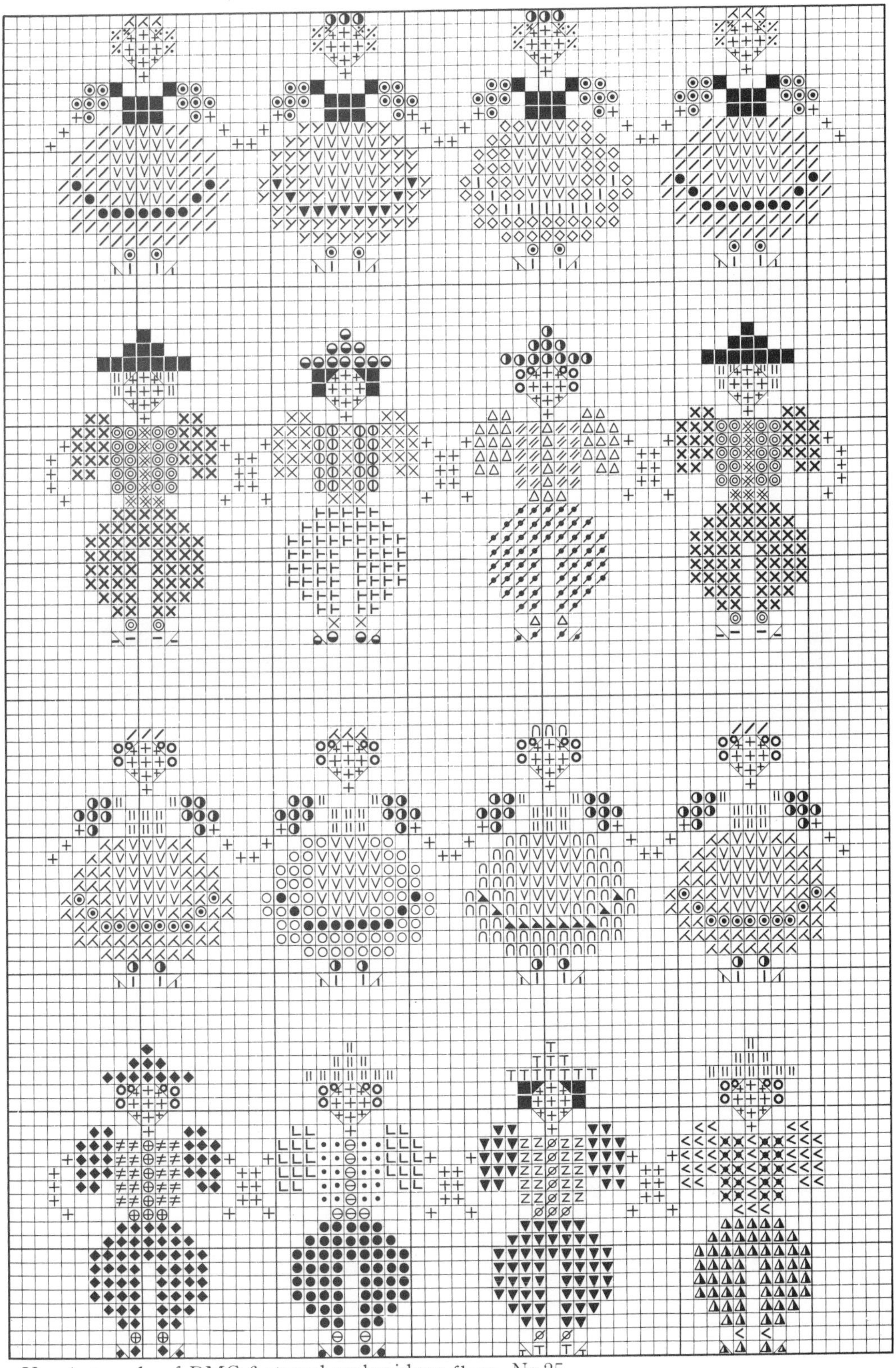

Use 4 strands of DMC 6-strand embroidery floss, No.25.

【Reds】 ⁄ = 3688 ● = 326 ◑ = 666 L = 602 ⊖ = 605 • = 892 【Yellows】 ◇ = 445 △ = 307

⌀ = 971 ⫽ = 972 ▲ = 741 ⋈ = 743 < = 744 【Browns】 + = 950 ⁒ = 407 I = 402 II = 300

◉ = 435 ○ = 976 ◆ = 838 ≠ = 841 ⊕ = 842 【Violets】 ◓ = 550 ⊢ = 552 Φ = 209 ⨯ = 211

【Greens】 ✖ = 911 ◎ = 704 ⋇ = 472 − = 987 ∩ = 966 ◣ = 912 【Blues】 ⊙ = 826 ⋌ = 827

Y = 597 ▼ = 930 Z = 518 ø = 519 【Grey】 T = 535 【Black】 ■ = 310 【White】 V

How to work Half Cross

 Instructions on page 42.

Instructions on page 43.

Use 4 strands of DMC 6-strand embroidery floss, No.25.

【Reds】 II=309 ●=666 V=963 ◢=817 ◐=946 I=351 ◇=353 •=602 ◒=606
【Yellows】 ⊣=972 Z=725 ⧅=307 ⊖=745 【Browns】 ∩=739 ◣=801 ⋰=402 【Violets】 ⌟=210
▲=552 ▼=553 ⊕=554 【Greens】 ✕=704 ◉=469 ╲=471 ⊥=992 ↘=701 【Blues】 ◎=996
■=939 ⋋=334 ○=800 ◘=798 △=828 【Black】 ◆=310 【Ecru】 ⦰ 【White】 +

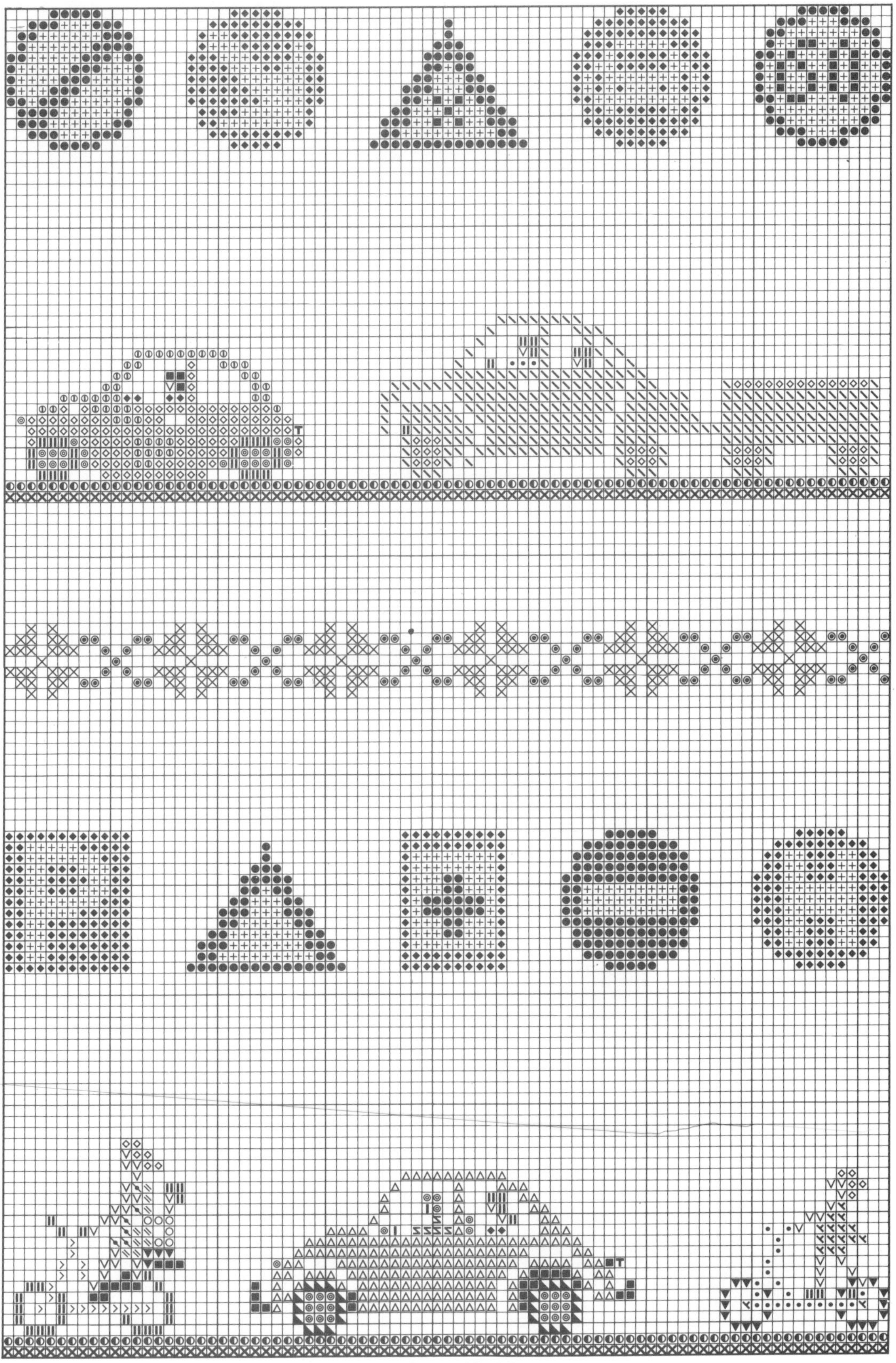

Use 4 strands of DMC 6-strand embroidery floss, No.25.

【Reds】 ● = 321 • = 605 T = 947 ◎ = 817 ⧅ = 335 【Yellows】 ◇ = 743 ☒ = 972 I = 725

【Browns】 ◎ = 435 ⦶ = 437 II = 801 ╲ = 976 > = 842 V = 945 【Violets】 ▼ = 553 ○ = 554 【Greens】 ◐ = 699

✖ = 890 ◣ = 500 △ = 703 【Blues】 ◆ = 517 ⧄ = 775 Σ = 926 ⬊ = 3325 【Black】 ■ = 310 【White】 +

MERRY-GO-ROUND

 Instructions on page 46.

Instructions on page 47.

Use 4 strands of DMC 6-strand embroidery floss, No.25. unless otherwise indicated.

【Reds】 ▲=321 V=761 •=891 ●=900 ⁄=962 ◆=3350 【Yellows】 Z=725 Y=740 ✕=742
//=743 O=744 【Browns】 ⋌=437 X=632 △=738 L=783 II=919 ◎=921 O=976
【Violets】 Φ=3041 <=3042 【Greens】 ⊢=833 −=906 ◢=909 ⊙=912 【Blue】 ◑=806
【Greys】 /=452 ∩=453 ⊖=844 【Ecru】 +

Use 4 strands of DMC 6-strand embroidery floss, No.25.

【Reds】 • = 603 ⁙ = 605 ╲ = 606 ● = 666 V = 819 ◉ = 3328 【Yellows】 ◇ = 307 ‖ = 741 O = 971
【Brown】 ⊣ = 780 【Violets】 Z = 209 > = 210 X = 211 【Greens】 ┘ = 704 ◣ = 830
【Blues】 ◎ = 800 ↘ = 826

 Instructions on page 50.

Instructions on page 51.

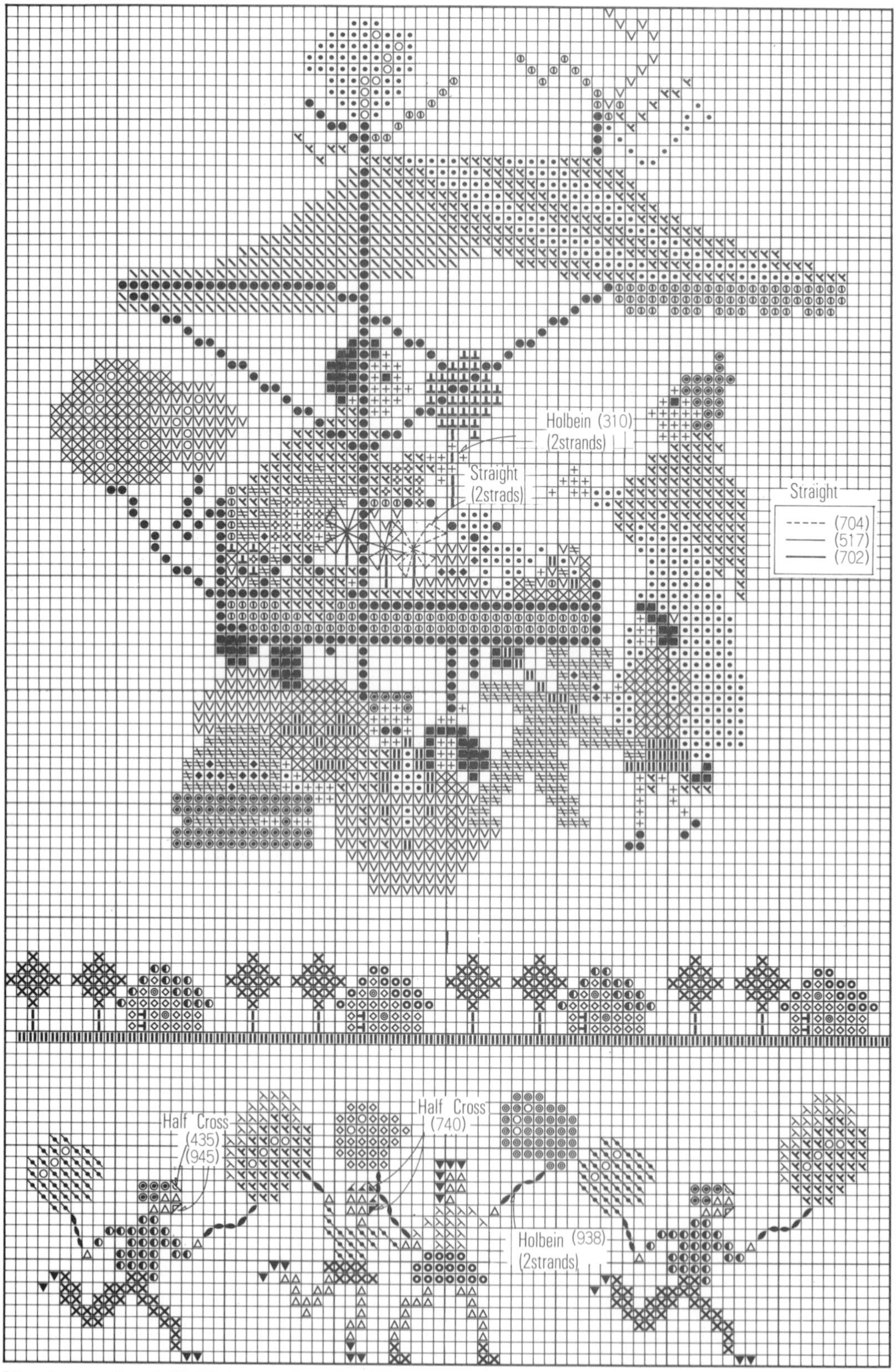

Use 4 strands of DMC 6-strand embroidery floss, No.25 unless otherwise indicated.

【Reds】 ⊥=600 ⧹=602 ●=606 +=818 •=956 ◐=304 【Yellows】 ◇=307 V=726 Φ=741
◢=740 ◣=742 【Browns】 ◉=435 ┫=434 ◇=437 ▮=977 ▼=938 △=945 【Violet】 \=210
【Greens】 ‖=702 ☒=704 ✖=3347 ⋋=954 【Blues】 ◆=517 ≠=519 ◎=813 ○=825
【Black】 ■=310 【White】 ○

Use 4 strands of DMC 6-strand embroidery floss, No.25 unless otherwise indicated.

【Reds】 ▼=602 ☒=605 •=891 ●=321 ◒=600 ⊞=818 【Yellows】 ◈=725 ┘=740 ◥=742 ○=973 ⊕=743 ⁘=972 ⊖=726 【Browns】 ◉=435 ◎=437 ◢=920 >=922 V=945 ∩=921

【Violets】 ┫=553 ◐=718 ╲=210 【Greens】 ⊙=703 ‖=912 ✖=3347 ≠=704 ⋋=954

【Blues】 ▮=799 ⦶=806 ▲=807 ⧅=813 ◣=825 Σ=826 【Black】 ■=310

 Instructions on page 54.

Instructions on page 55.

【Reds】
● = 349 ◐ = 601
▼ = 815 • = 947
⅃ = 3688 ☒ = 3689
◆ = 892

【Yellows】
≠ = 307 + = 740

【Browns】
⊖ = 402 ◣ = 434
∩ = 739 ◘ = 783
Y = 841 ▬ = 842

【Violets】
◢ = 208 ◇ = 209
○ = 211 ◉ = 917

【Greens】
▲ = 319 ‖ = 700
△ = 704 ✧ = 907
⋋ = 472 ✖ = 581
┫ = 911 ⫽ = 912

【Blues】
Σ = 807 T = 826

【Greys】
I = 318 ⊠ = 415
⊥ = 414

【Black】
■ = 310

【Ecru】
V

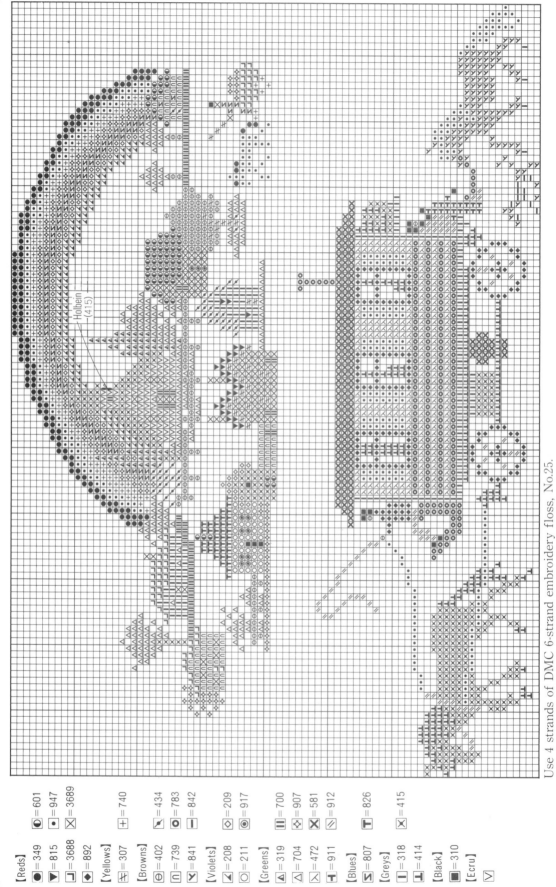

Use 4 strands of DMC 6-strand embroidery floss, No.25.

【Reds】
◑ = 309　◎ = 335
● = 347　L = 3326

【Yellows】
Z = 726　• = 741

【Browns】
∩ = 422　< = 435
II = 921　V = 945

【Violets】
⊠ = 209　⋌ = 210

【Greens】
Φ = 911　X = 992
△ = 993　/ = 469
⊙ = 703　// = 907
○ = 3348

【Blues】
◣ = 806　o = 807
◇ = 519

【Grey】
⊠ = 762

【Black】
■ = 310

【White】
+

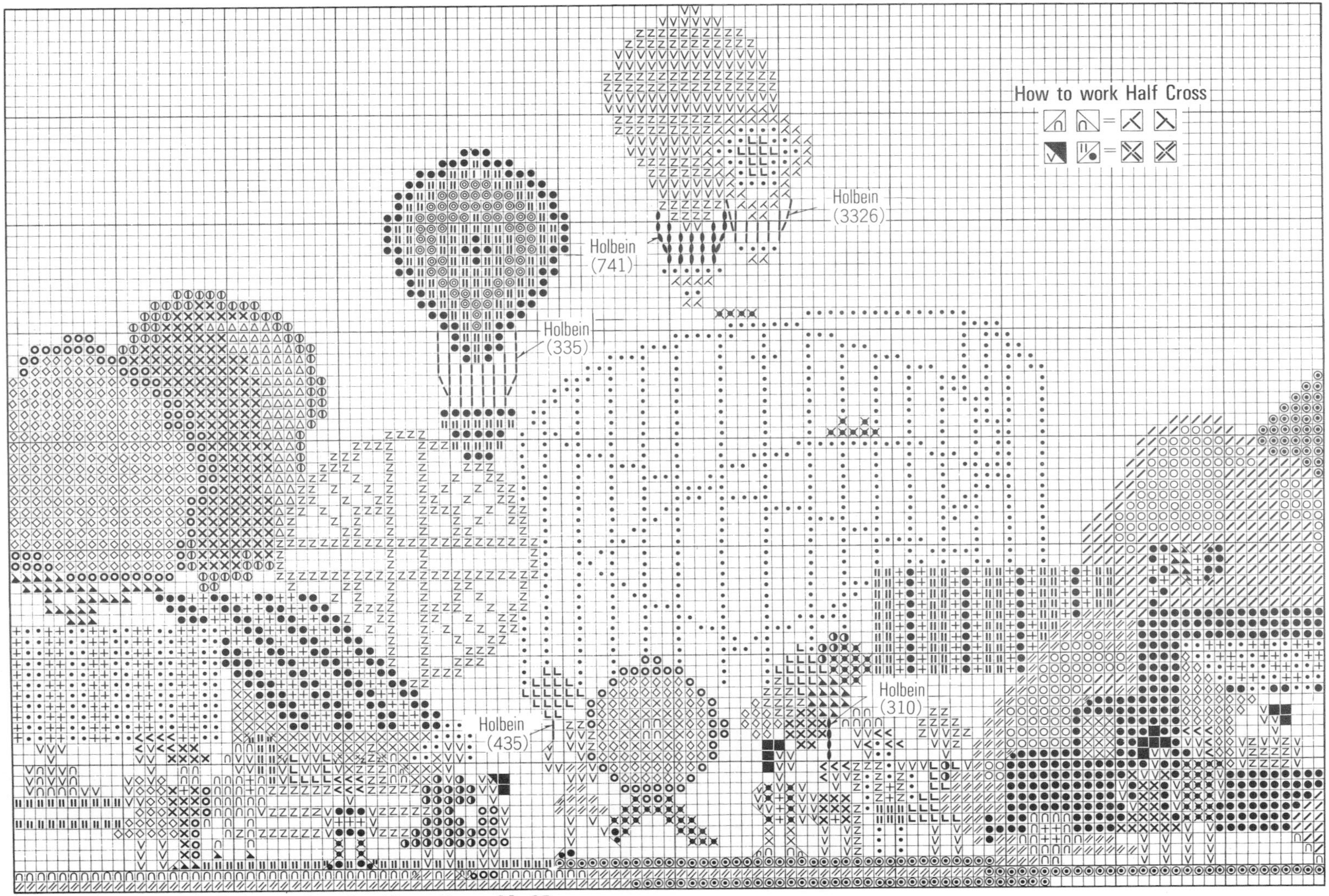

Use 4 strands of DMC 6-strand embroidery floss, No.25.

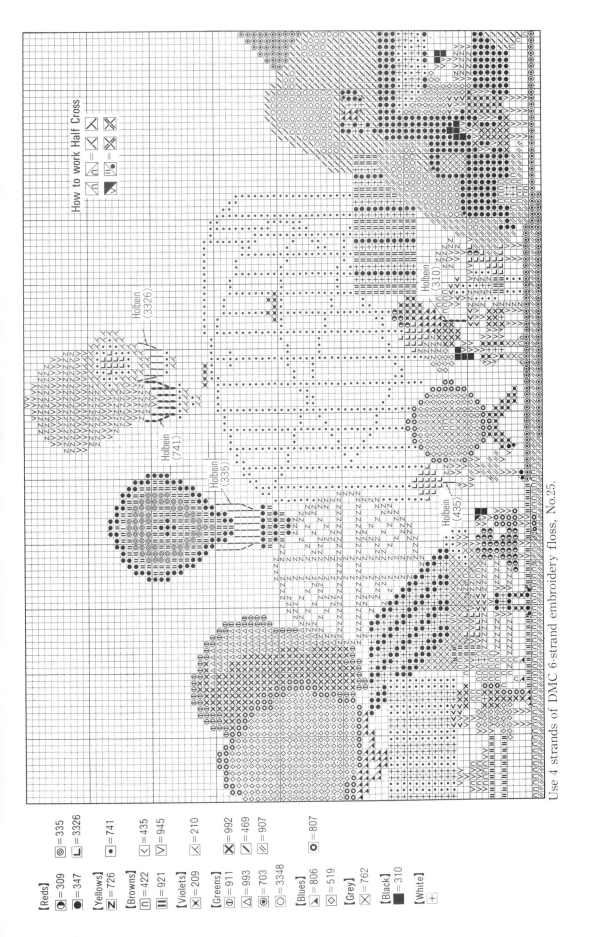

Carnival

Instructions on page 58.

Instructions on page 59.

Use 4 strands of DMC 6-strand embroidery floss, No.25 unless otherwise indicated.

Common to p.p.58-59. 【Reds】 ▼=349 ┛=350 ●=600 ⁙=602 ◒=666 ⊡=760 ◣=814 V=818 ⨪=894 ⧅=963 【Yellows】 >=307 ⊕=445 ⊘=726 Σ=970 Φ=972 【Browns】 △=402 ▲=433 T=434 ◎=611 I=783 ◥=841 ∠=920 ⋋=922 【Violets】 ∩=209 ◆=550 X=553

Use 4 strands of DMC 6-strand embroidery floss, No.25 unless otherwise indicated.

【Greens】 ⟐=472 ‖=702 ⊠=704 ◘=910 ◣=991 ◉=3013 【Blues】 ⊣=517 ⋎=518 ○=519

☒=813 ◐=824 ▬=924 【Greys】 ⊖=414 ◇=415 【Black】 ■=310 【White】 ⊞

 Instructions on page 62.

Instructions on page 63.

【Reds】

▐▌ = 335 ⧅ = 498

◉ = 600 ☒ = 605

⦶ = 900

【Yellow】

◇ = 973

【Violets】

△ = 209 ∩ = 316

⧅ = 553

【Browns】

■ = 300 ⧅ = 781

• = 783

【Blues】

● = 791 ┘ = 793

【Ecru】

∨

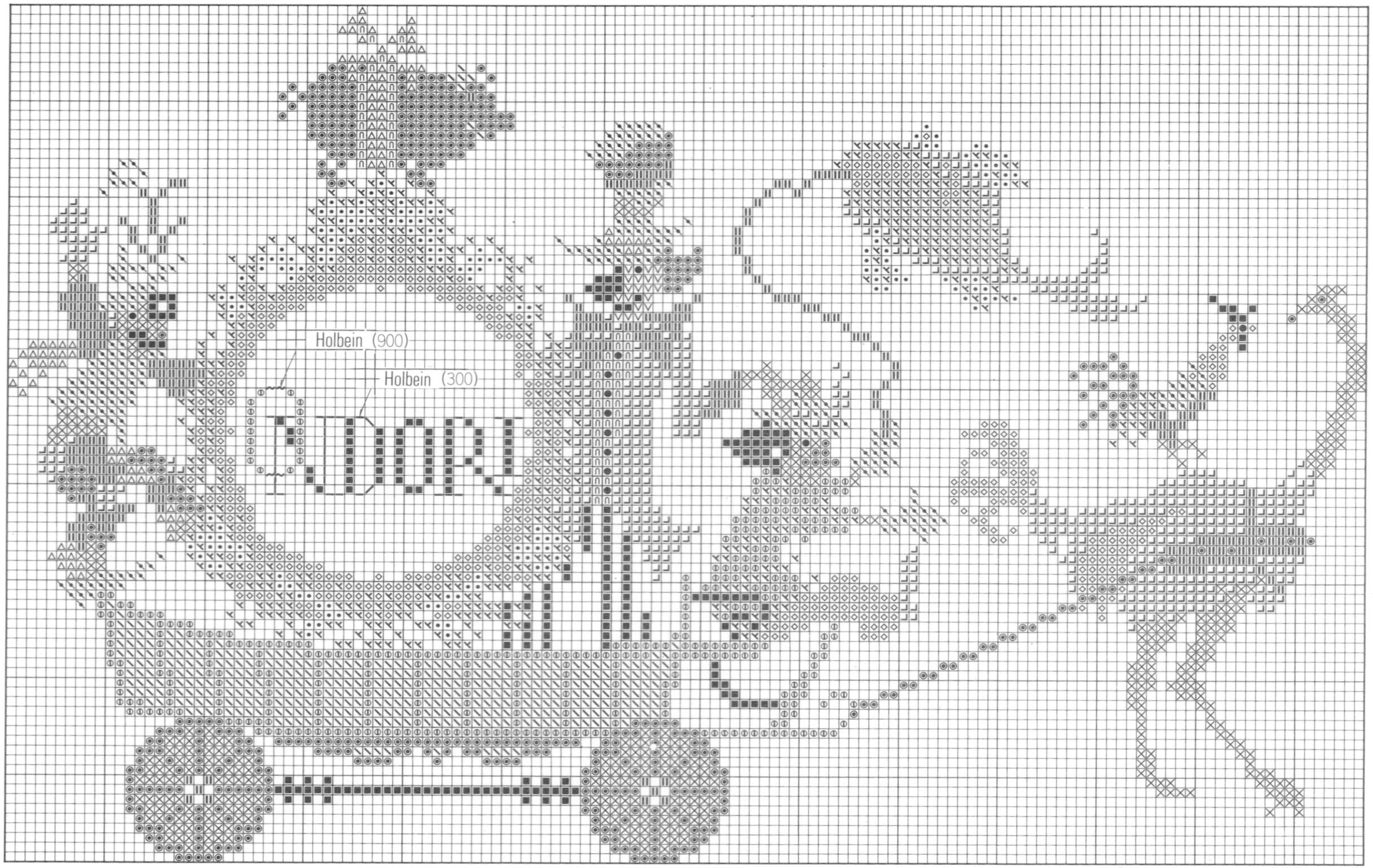

Use 3 strands of DMC 6-strand embroidery floss, No.25.

【Reds】
- ● = 326
- ⌟ = 335
- • = 776
- ╲ = 3326
- ‖ = 3685
- ☒ = 3689

【Yellows】
- ◉ = 740
- △ = 743
- ◇ = 972

【Browns】
- ☒ = 435
- ▼ = 801
- ◆ = 918
- V = 951
- > = 976

【Violet】
- ∩ = 210

【Greens】
- ✓ = 912
- ◢ = 943
- ○ = 954

【Blues】
- ◐ = 806
- ↘ = 807

【Black】
- ■ = 310

【White】
- +

Use 3 strands of DMC 6-strand embroidery floss, No.25.

 Instructions on page 66.

Instructions on page 67.

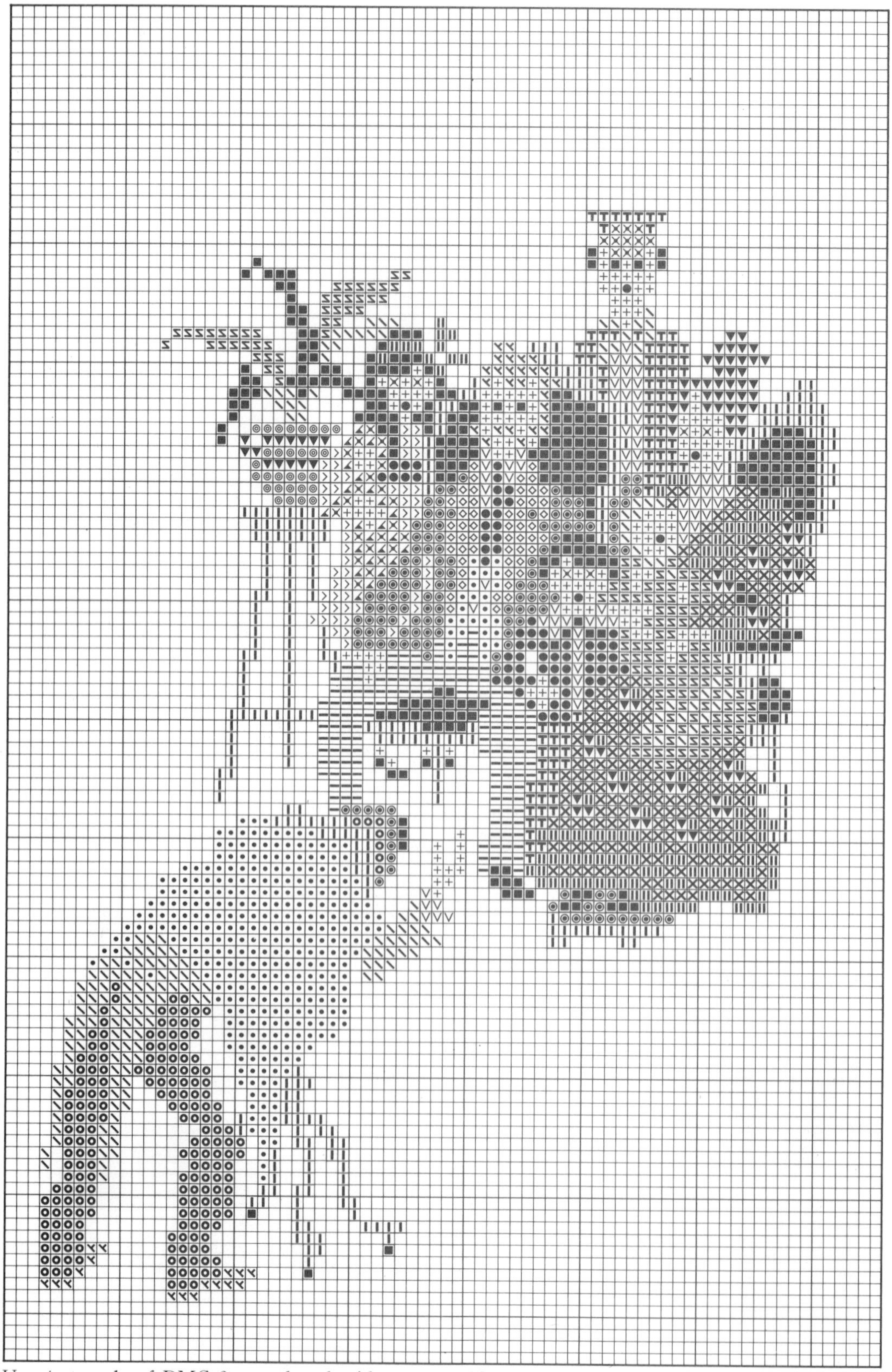

Use 4 strands of DMC 6-strand embroidery floss, No.25.

【Reds】 ‖ = 498 ● = 666 + = 761 ▼ = 946 > = 3328 【Yellows】 ◇ = 726 ◎ = 740 【Browns】 I = 420

ϒ = 632 【Violet】 • = 553 【Greens】 — = 734 ✕ = 911 Z = 955 ＼ = 3347 【Blues】 ✕ = 519

T = 798 ∠ = 799 【Greys】 ◉ = 414 O = 648 【Black】 ■ = 310 【Ecru】 V

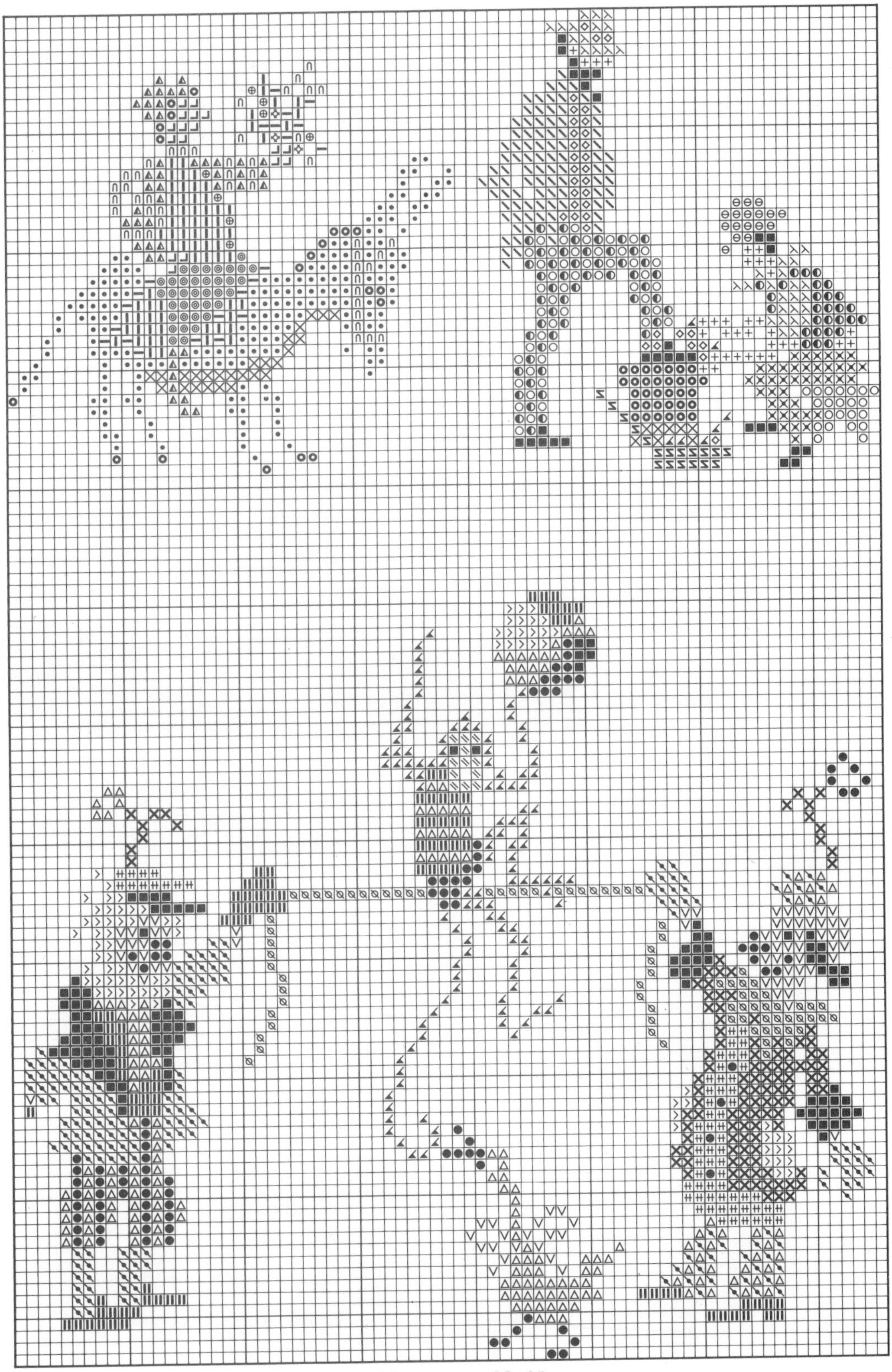

Use 4 strands of DMC 6-strand embroidery floss, No.25.

【Reds】 ▬=309 ┘=353 ▌=892 ◐=947 ◥=335 ●=815 V=3689 【Yellows】 ∩=307 ⊕=740 ◇=725 ⊘=745 △=973 【Browns】 ◢=869 ○=977 ⑊=842 【Violets】 ◎=209 ▲=718

【Greens】 ⟡=966 Z=833 λ=954 ╲=989 ✕=3348 >=472 ✖=580

【Blues】 ⊖=747 ‖=797 ♯=806 【Greys】 •=318 ◘=414 ╳=415 【Black】 ■=310 【Ecru】 +

Zoo

 Instructions on page 70.

Instructions on page 71.

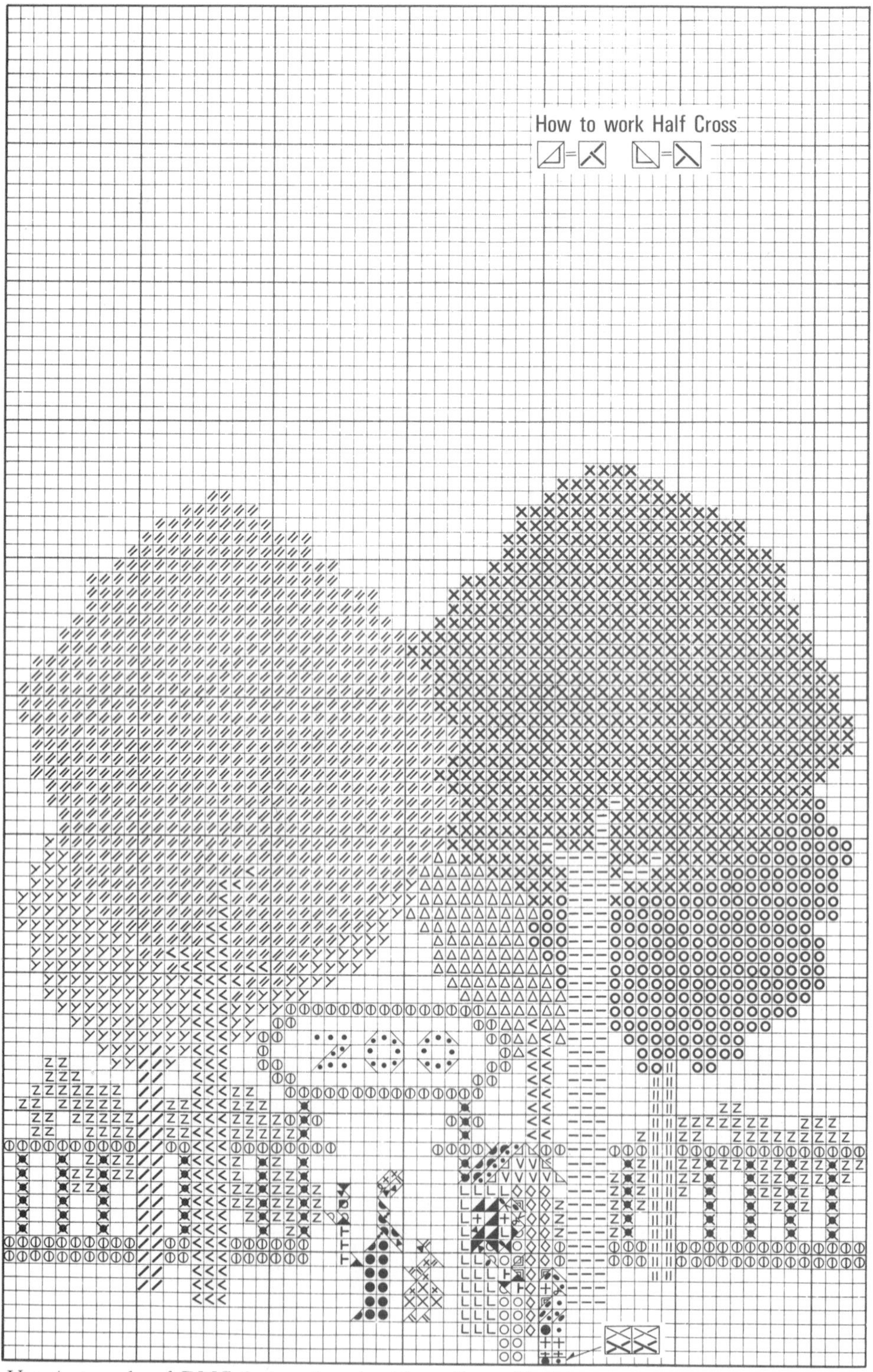

Use 4 strands of DMC 6-strand embroidery floss, No.25.

【Reds】 ● = 602 · = 603 V = 605 【Yellows】 // = 444 Z = 726 Y = 742 △ = 744 X = 970

【Browns】 O = 783 / = 841 + = 950 【Violets】 ⊢ = 208 ○ = 209 【Greens】 ✖ = 581 < = 733

【Blues】 ◇ = 747 ✖ = 799 ⦶ = 800 ◢ = 806 L = 807 【Greys】 — = 318 || = 414

Half Cross { = 600 = 602 = 603 = 605 = 606 = 208 = 209 = 733 = 718 = 747
= 799 = 800 = 806 = 807 = 839 = 915 = 947 = 950 = 970

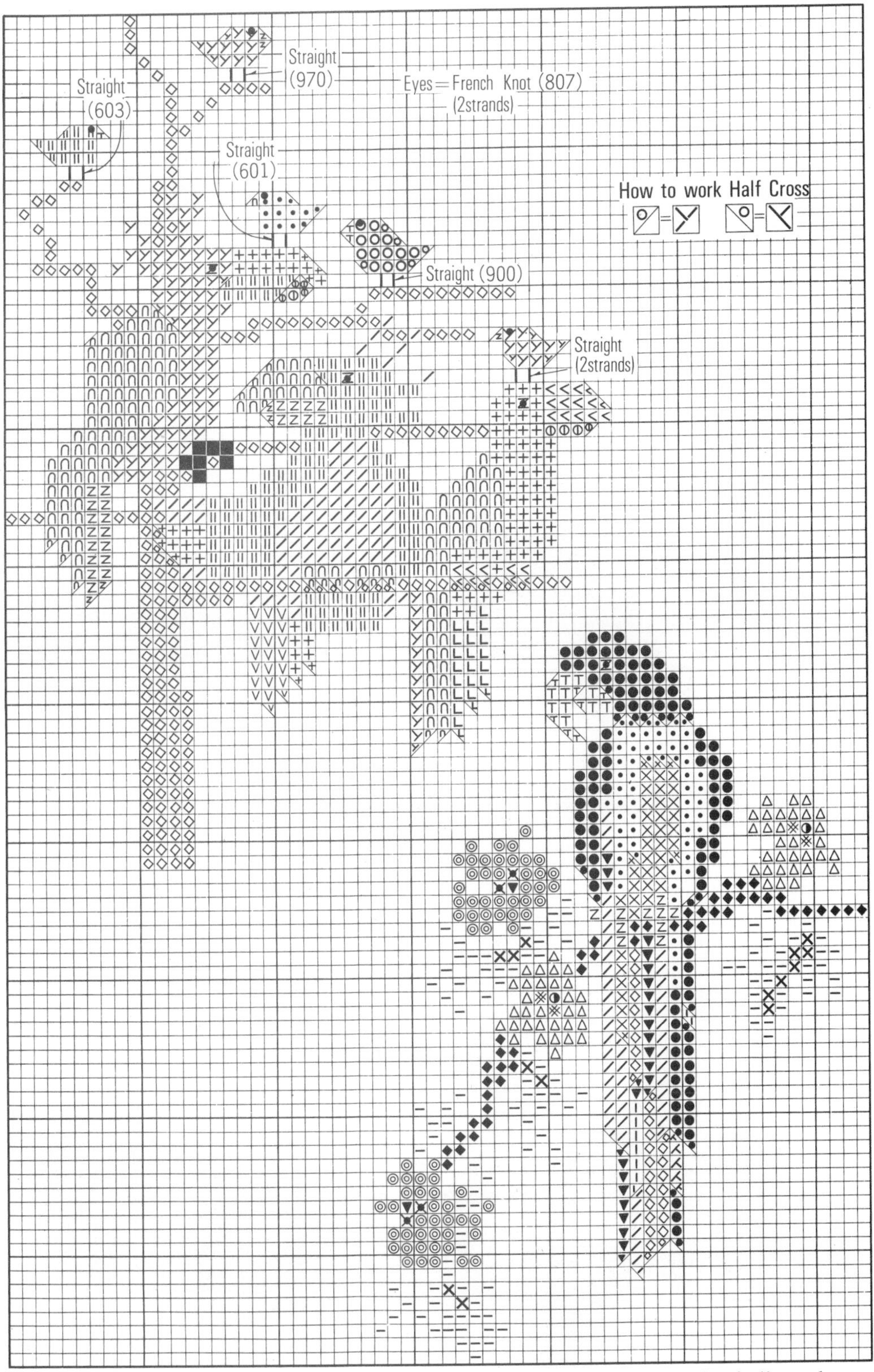

Use 5 strands of DMC 6-strand embroidery floss, No.25 unless otherwise indicated.

【Reds】 ▼ = 304 ✖ = 309 ◑ = 326 ⋇ = 335 ⦶ = 600 • = 601 < = 602 II = 603 V = 604 + = 605 ■ = 606 △ = 776 ○ = 900 ╱ = 947 ◎ = 3326

【Yellows】 Z = 444 ╳ = 740 T = 741 ⋂ = 742 L = 744 Y = 970

【Violets】 ◇ = 211 ⋌ = 552 I = 553 ● = 915

【Greens】 ◆ = 319 ✕ = 911 — = 993

 Instructions on page 74.

Instructions on page 75.

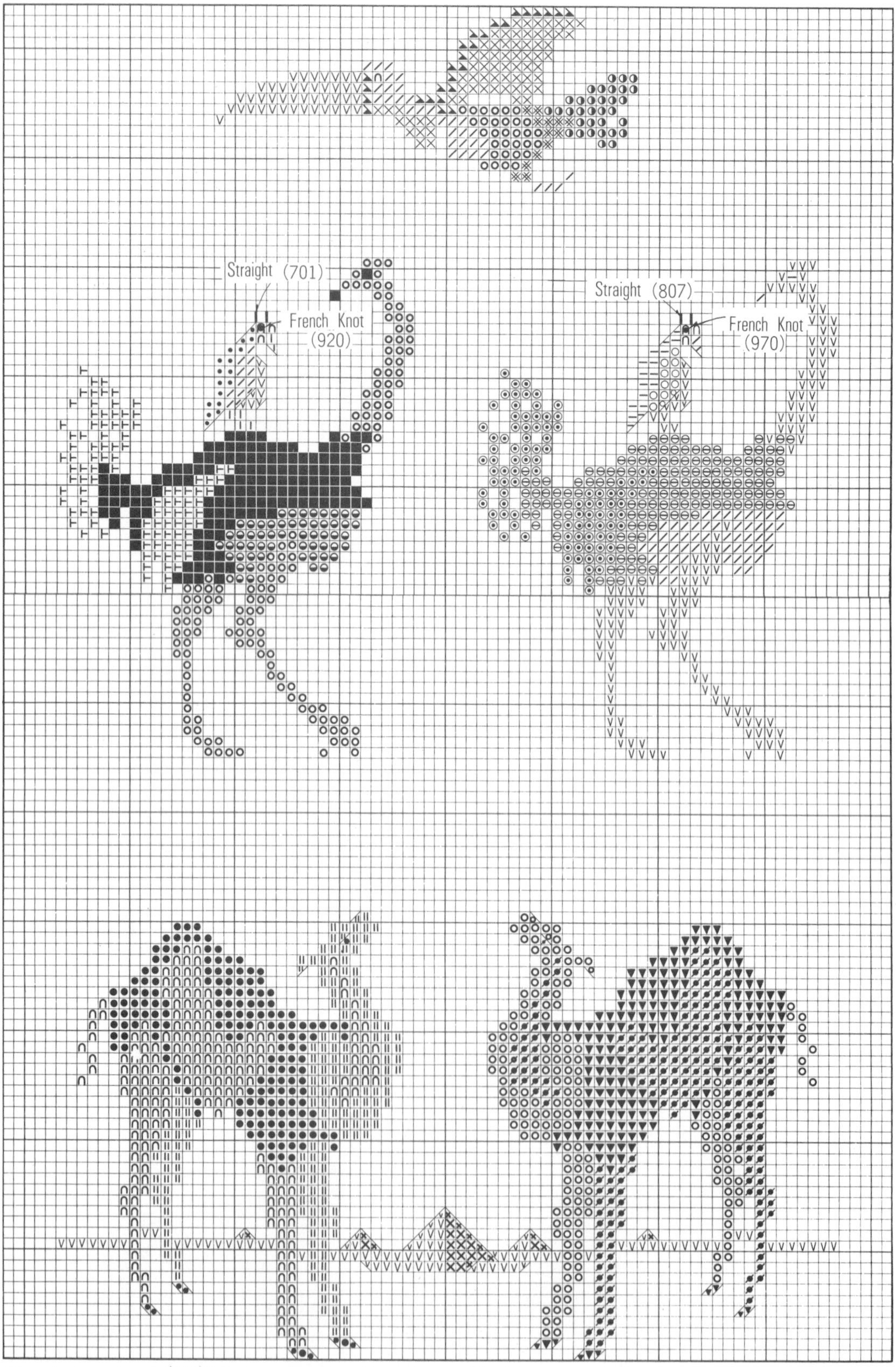

Use 4 strands of DMC 6-strand embroidery floss, No.25.

【Reds】 X = 776 ◑ = 600 ※ = 335 ⊢ = 3685 ⊙ = 666 ⊖ = 947 ⊘ = 304 ▼ = 902 【Yellows】 V = 742
/ = 970 ✖ = 971 【Brown】 | = 920 【Violet】 O = 718 【Greens】 • = 701 O = 472 ● = 991
【Blues】 ◣ = 797 ∩ = 807 ◒ = 820 − = 597 II = 517 【Black】 ■ = 310 How to work ⁄ = X ◣ = ⟍
Half Cross

Use 4 strands of DMC 6-strand embroidery floss, No.25.

【Reds】 ◎ = 666 ⊡ = 3326 ○ = 604 【Yellows】 Z = 726 ◎ = 741 ◇ = 740 【Browns】 ◆ = 898
∕ = 435 + = 738 − = 782 Φ = 436 ∠ = 433 ∕ = 3032 I = 920 V = 729 【Violets】 ● = 327
⊠ = 553 ∕∕ = 3042 X = 552 【Greens】 ＜ = 966 II = 3012 【Blues】 ○ = 800 ▲ = 807
【Grey】 △ = 415 【Black】 ■ = 310 How to work Half Cross

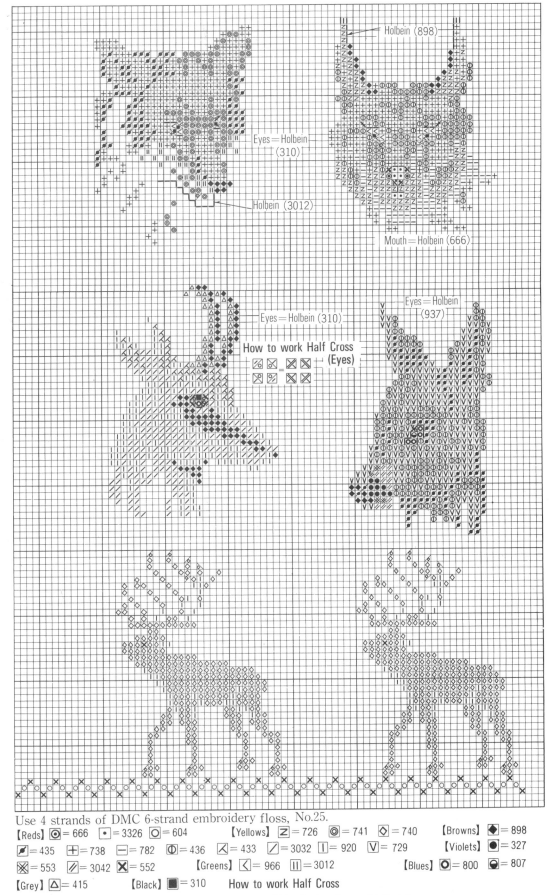

Ibid. refer to p.74;except indicated

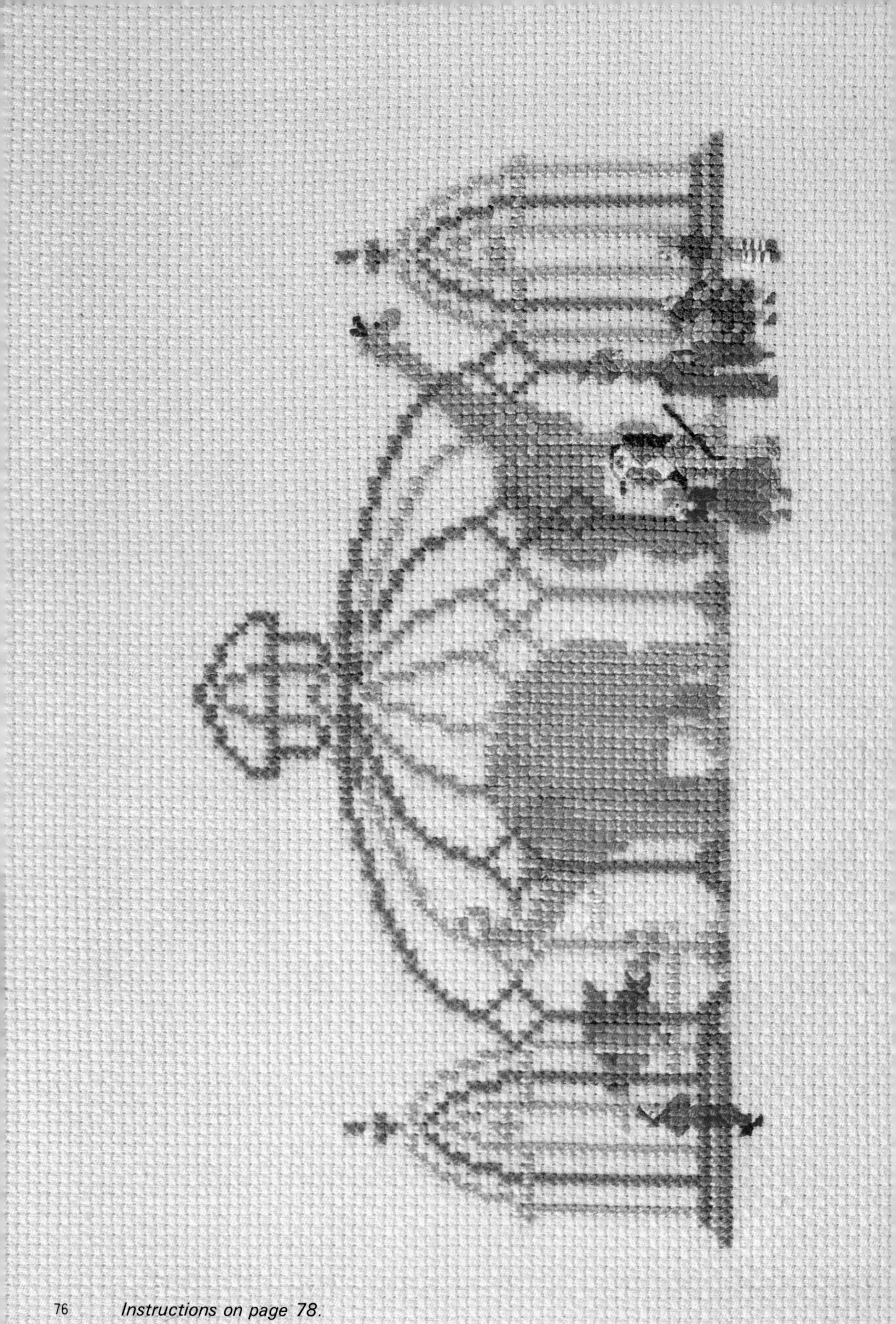

 Instructions on page 78.

Instructions on page 79.

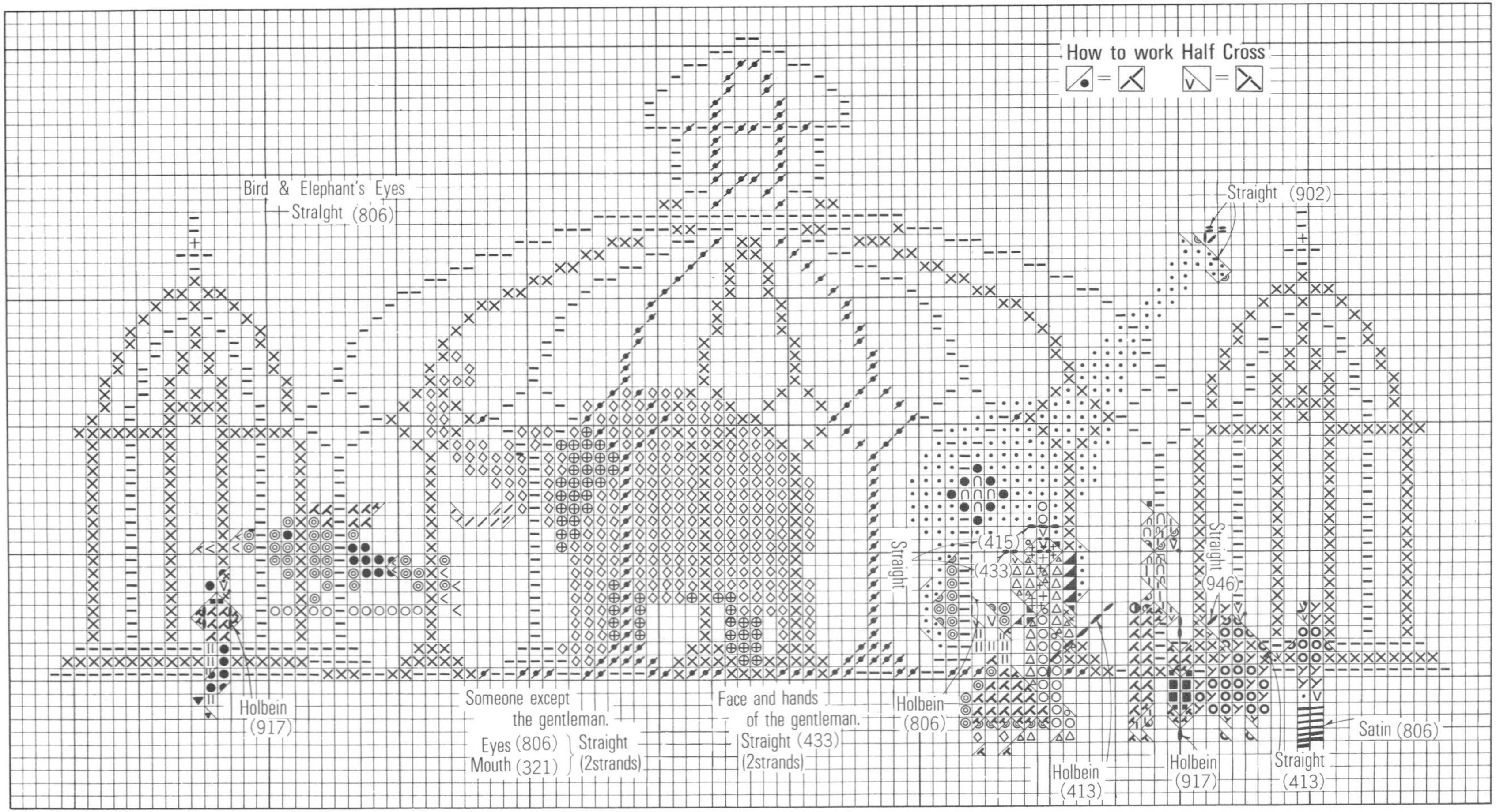

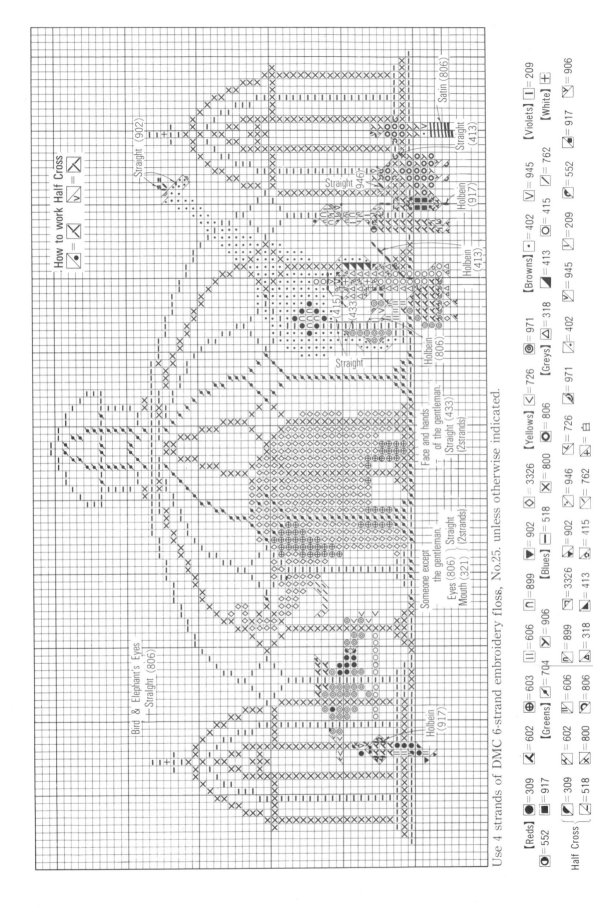

Use 4 strands of DMC 6-strand embroidery floss, No.25. unless otherwise indicated.

【Reds】 [●] = 309 [⋌] = 602 [⊕] = 603 [||] = 606 [∩] = 899 [▼] = 902 [◇] = 3326 【Yellows】 [<] = 726 [◎] = 971 【Browns】 [·] = 402 [V] = 945 【Violets】 [I] = 209
[◑] = 552 [■] = 917 【Greens】 [⁄] = 704 [Y] = 906 【Blues】 [—] = 518 [X] = 800 [O] = 806 【Greys】 [△] = 318 [◢] = 413 [○] = 415 [/] = 762 【White】 [+]

Half Cross { [half-filled square] = 309 [⋌] = 602 [||] = 606 [∩] = 899 [half square, 3326] = 3326 [▼] = 902 [half square, 946] = 946 [<] = 726 [◎] = 971 [·] = 402 [V] = 945 [I] = 209 [◑] = 552 [■] = 917 [Y] = 906
[—] = 518 [X] = 800 [O] = 806 [△] = 318 [◢] = 413 [○] = 415 [/] = 762 [+] = 白

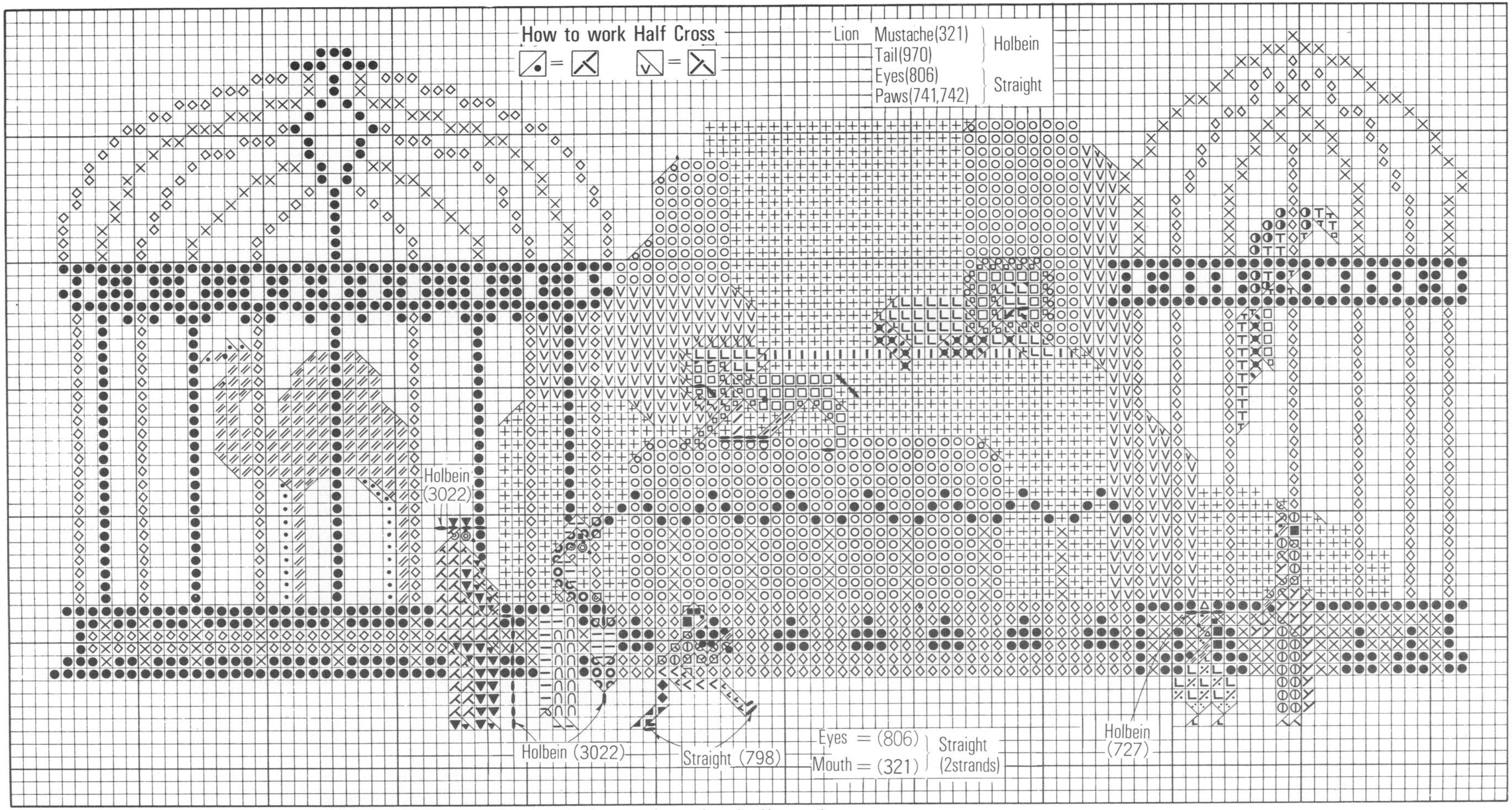

Use 4 strands of DMC 6-strand embroidery floss, No.25 unless otherwise indicated.

【Reds】 ● = 309 　X = 605 　◎ = 776 　⊠ = 946 　◇ = 3326 　【Yellows】 △ = 727 　/ = 741 　□ = 742 　⁒ = 743 　L = 970 　【Browns】 · = 402 　■ = 612

// = 738 　【Violets】 ◑ = 208 　I = 209 　+ = 211 　○ = 554 　T = 917 　【Greens】 V = 504 　Y = 906 　Φ = 907 　【Blues】 — = 518 　∩ = 519 　◆ = 797

< = 798 　◉ = 806 　【Greys】 ▼ = 3022 　ㅅ = 3023

Half Cross { (309) = 309 　(605) = 605 　(776) = 776 　(946) = 946 　(3326) = 3326 　(727) = 727 　(741) = 741 　(742) = 742 　(743) = 743 　(970) = 970 　(402) = 402 　(612) = 612 　(738) = 738 　(208) = 208
(209) = 209 　(211) = 211 　(554) = 554 　(917) = 917 　(504) = 504 　(906) = 906 　(907) = 907 　(518) = 518 　(519) = 519 　(797) = 797 　(798) = 798 　(806) = 806 　(3022) = 3022 　(3023) = 3023 }

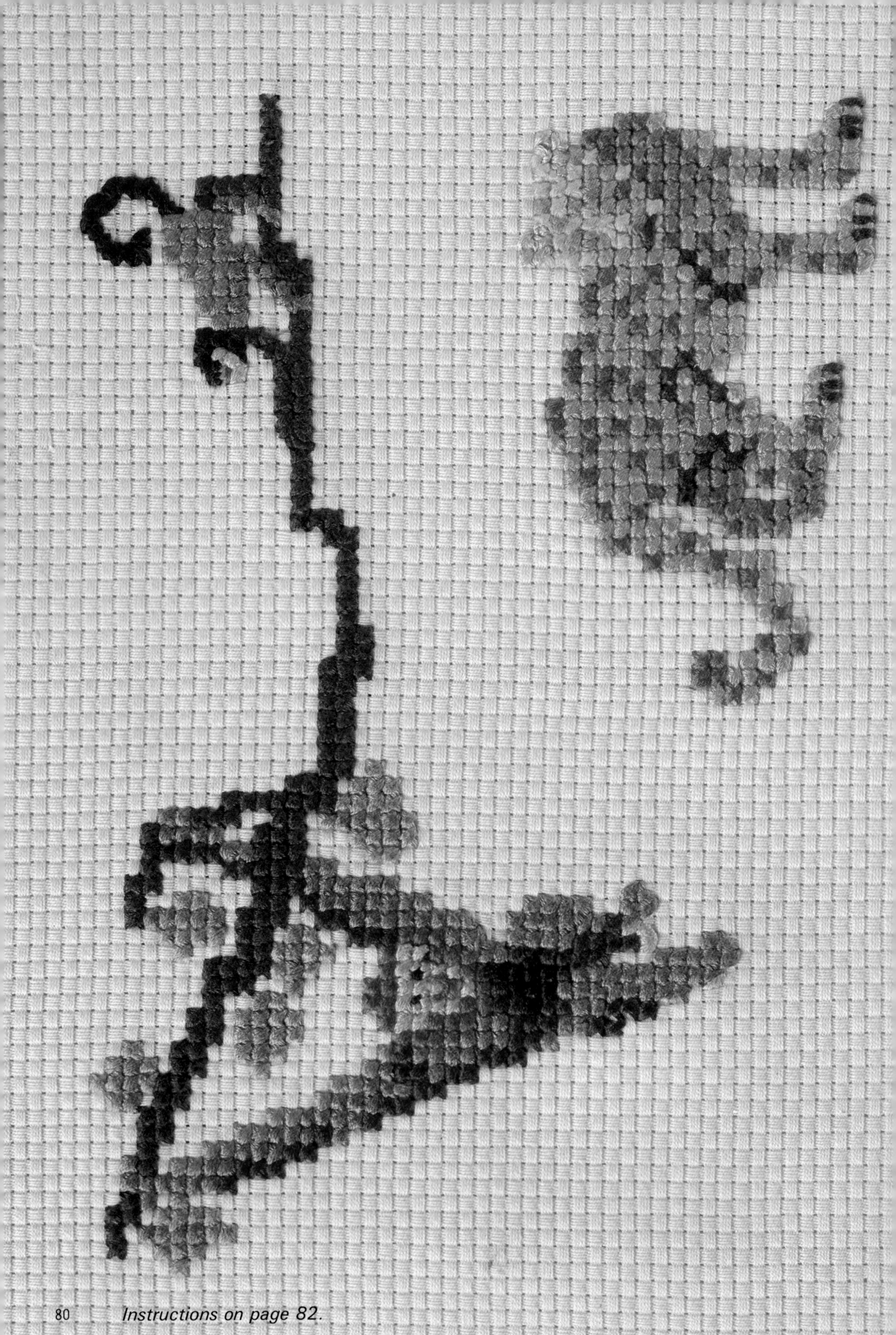

 Instructions on page 82.

Instructions on page 83.

【Red】
V = 605

【Yellows】
% = 971
+ = 972

【Browns】
⊢ = 301
/ = 436
◑ = 801
△ = 841
◆ = 938
X = 402
• = 976

【Greens】
O = 906
⟋ = 907
● = 986
< = 704

How to work
Half Cross
[illegible] = [illegible]
[illegible] = [illegible]

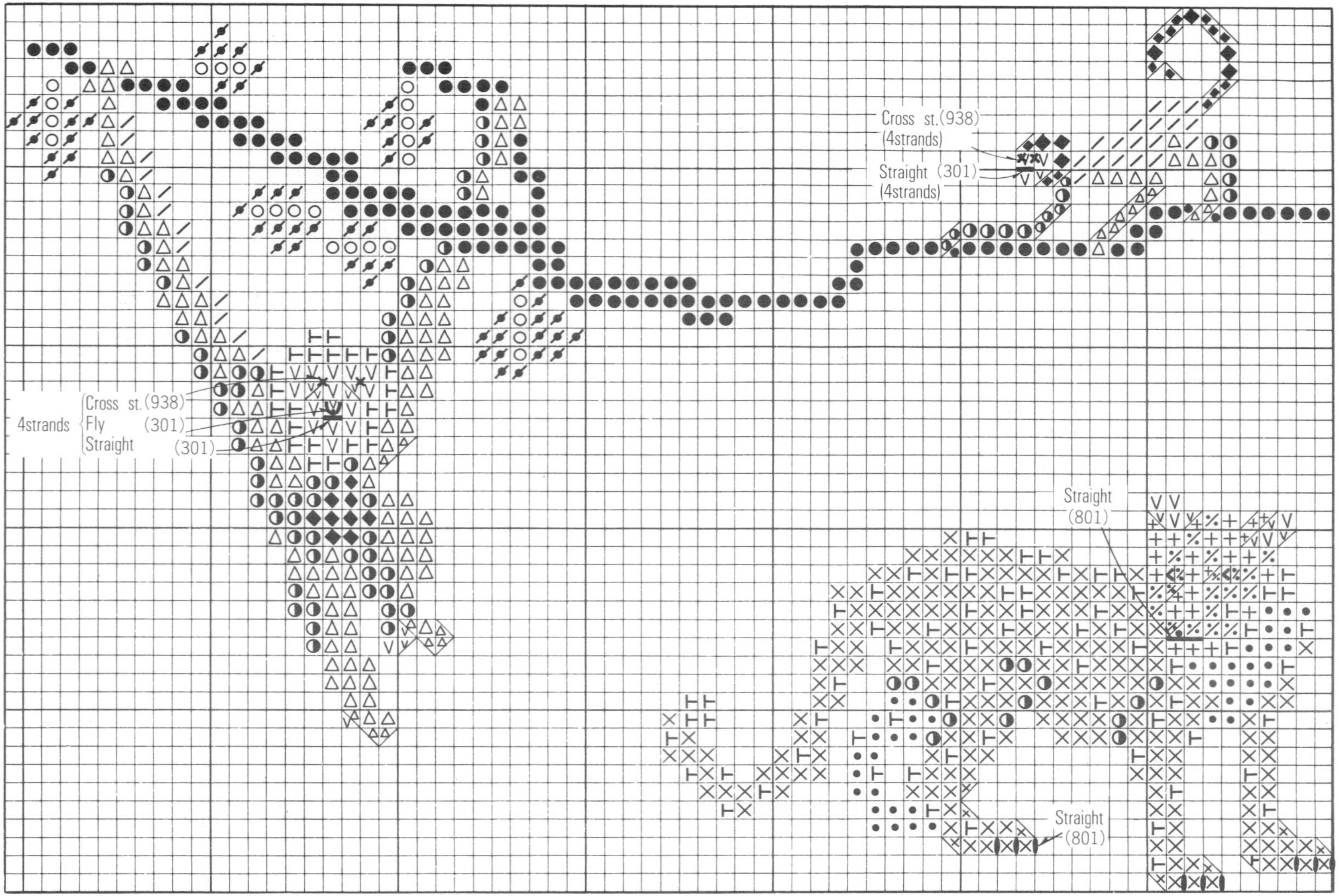

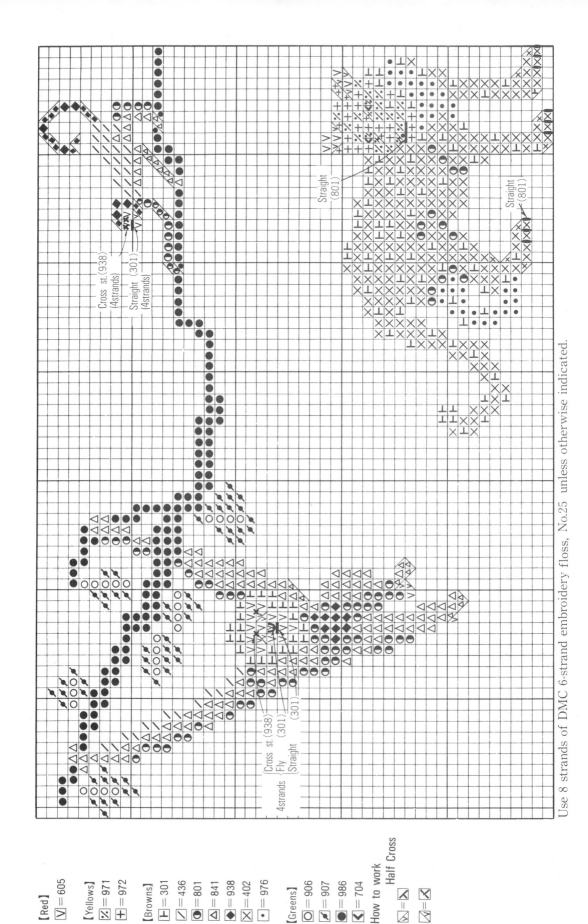

Use 8 strands of DMC 6-strand embroidery floss, No.25 unless otherwise indicated.

【Yellows】
◇ = 444
+ = 972

【Browns】
• = 435
◎ = 437
○ = 738
◆ = 938

【Green】
/ = 472

【Greys】
▼ = 317
✕ = 318
△ = 415

【Black】
■ = 310

How to work
Half Cross
See page 82.

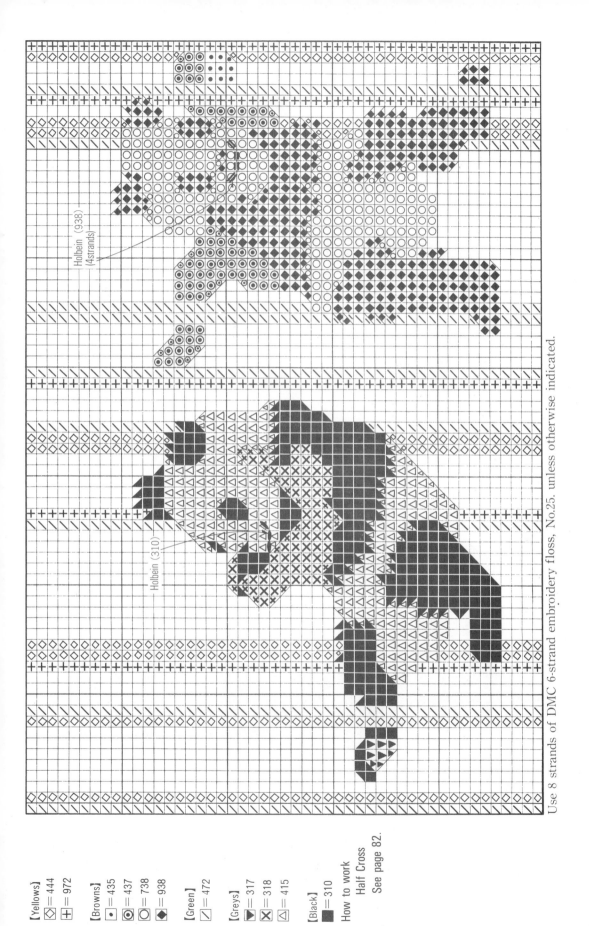

Use 8 strands of DMC 6-strand embroidery floss, No.25. unless otherwise indicated.

 Instructions on page 86.

Instructions on page 87.

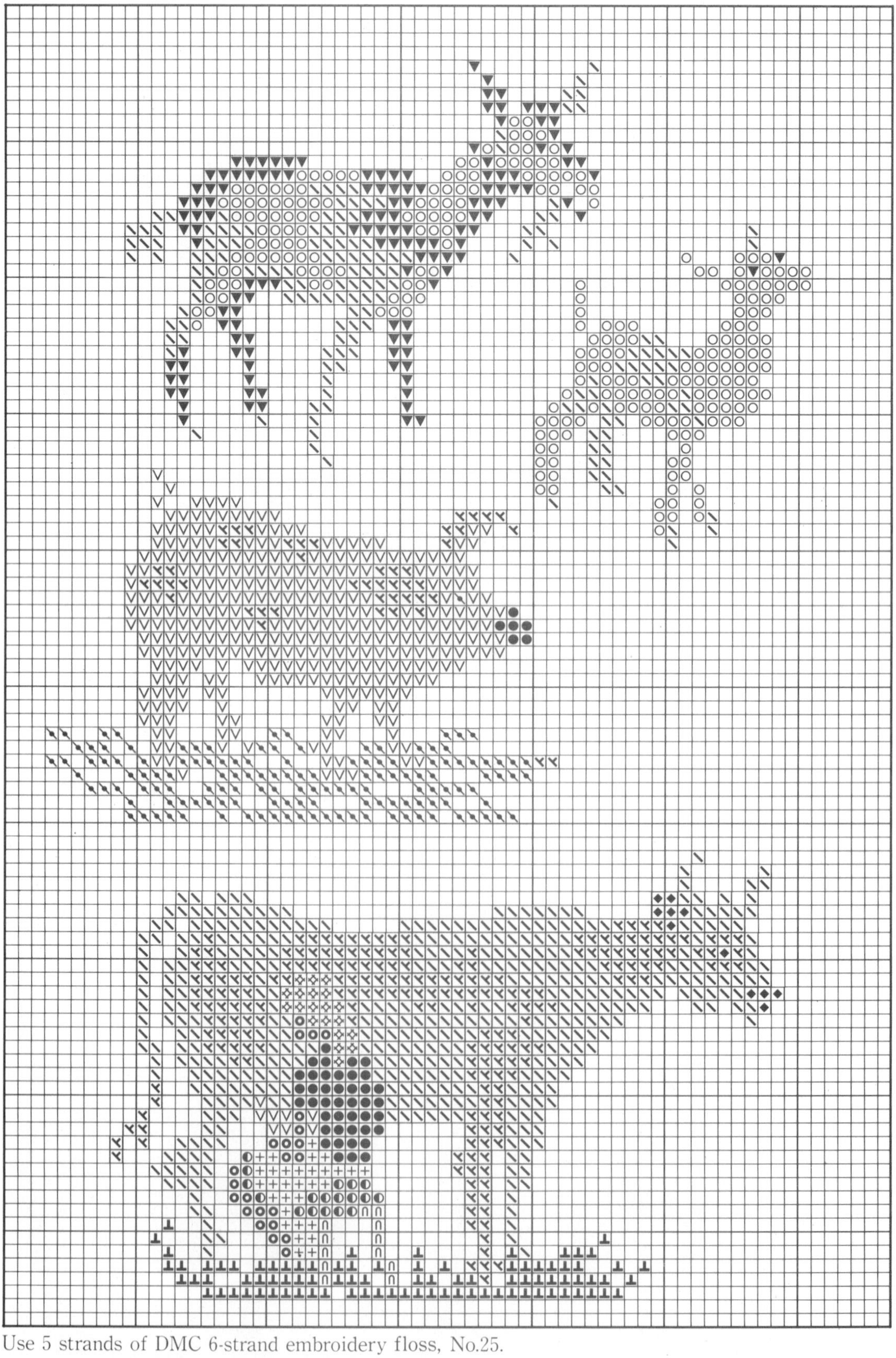

Use 5 strands of DMC 6-strand embroidery floss, No.25.

【Reds】 ●=309 V=3689 【Yellows】 ◘=740 ∩=742 【Browns】 ▼=433 ╲=436 ○=842 ⋌=434 ◆=898
【Greens】 ╲•=704 ┻=906 【Blues】 ◐=826 +=827 ✧=800

Use 5 strands of DMC 6-strand embroidery floss, No.25 unless otherwise indicated.

【Reds】 ●=309 ┫=892 V=3689 ■=666 ☒=899 【Browns】 ◉=801 ⋎=434 △=644

【Greens】 ◣=704 ✖=905 ‖=909 【Blue】 ◇=800

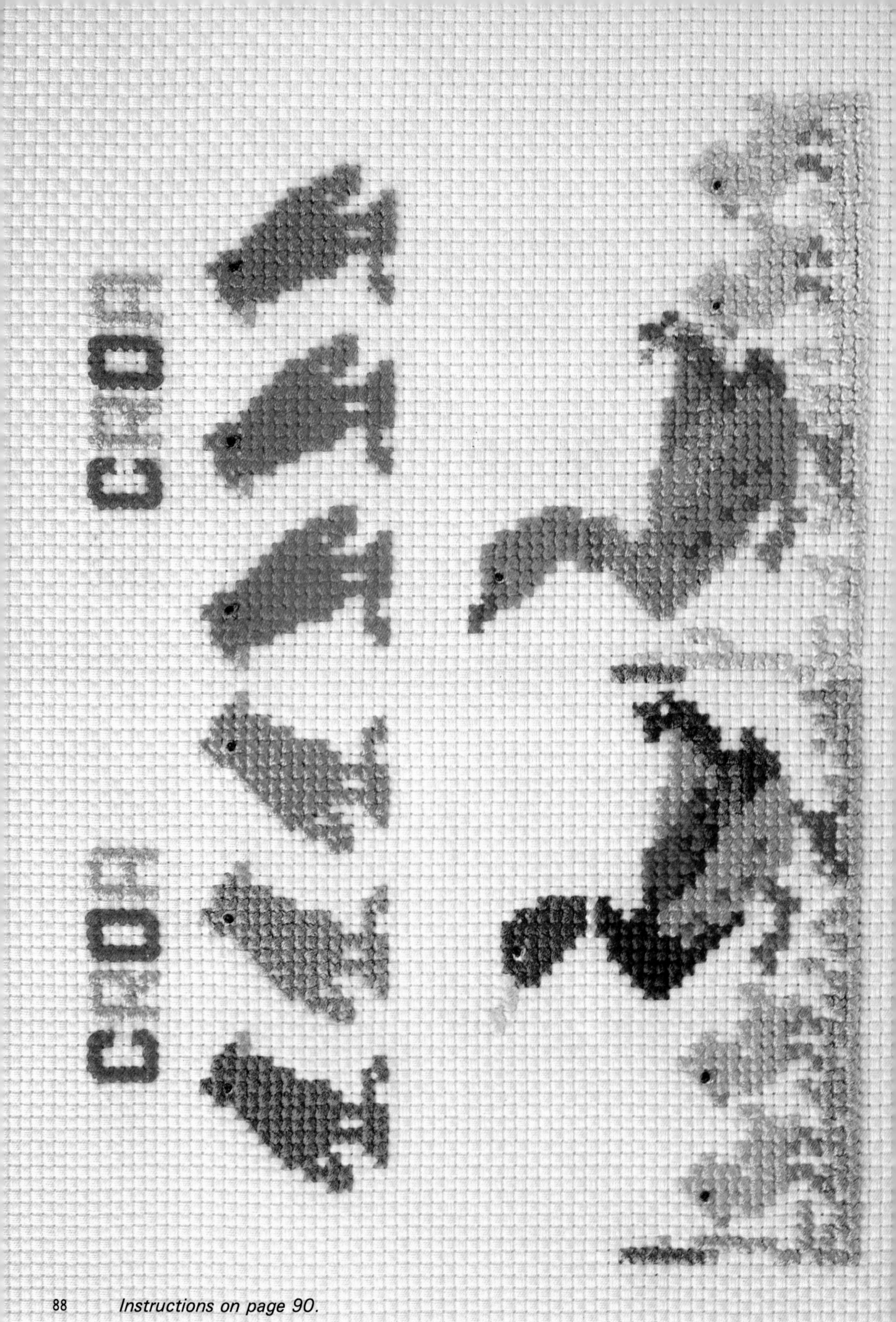

 Instructions on page 90.

Instructions on page 91.

【Reds】

- ○ = 3326
- ◆ = 304
- ‖ = 335
- • = 899
- ◎ = 946
- ⊙ = 602
- ◐ = 326
- ⊠ = 606
- ▼ = 902
- ◇ = 947

【Yellows】

- — = 742
- V = 741
- ⊥ = 970

【Browns】

- Σ = 921
- ⊖ = 945

【Violets】

- ■ = 917
- ◉ = 718
- Φ = 553
- ↘ = 209

【Greens】

- ╲ = 703
- ╳ = 472
- ┘ = 704
- ∩ = 912
- ✖ = 911
- ┤ = 581
- ⋎ = 909

【Blues】

- ⧅ = 799
- ◢ = 807

【Half Cross】

- ◢, ⧅ } = 917
- ⌀, ⧄ } = 3326

Use 5 strands of DMC 6-strand embroidery floss, No.25 unless otherwise indicated.

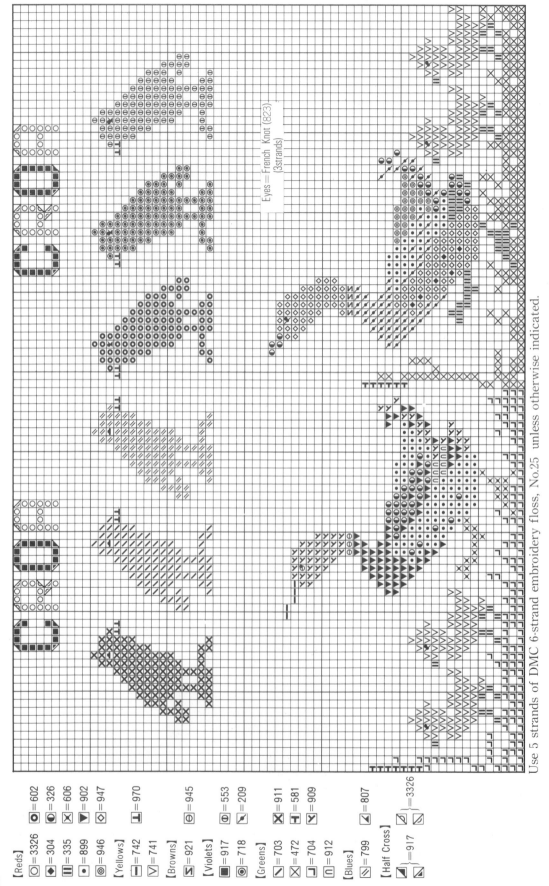

【Reds】
- ◐ = 321
- • = 761

【Yellows】
- + = 725
- △ = 973

【Browns】
- ∩ = 402
- ╲ = 433
- ⊙ = 434
- ◉ = 783
- ◢ = 801
- ■ = 938
- ⊠ = 976

【Violets】
- ● = 208
- ‖ = 209
- ◇ = 211

【Blues】
- Z = 800
- ↘ = 807

【Grey】
- Φ = 414

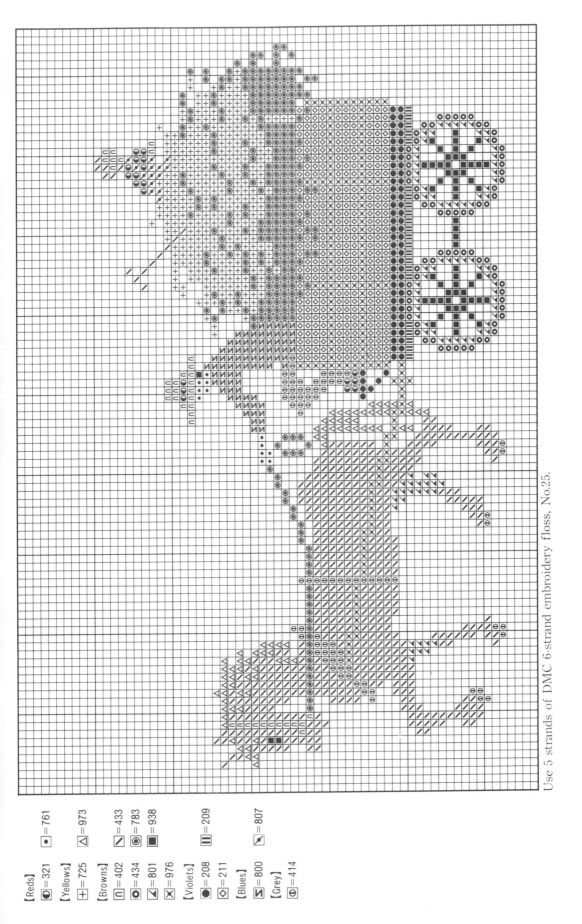

Use 5 strands of DMC 6-strand embroidery floss, No.25.

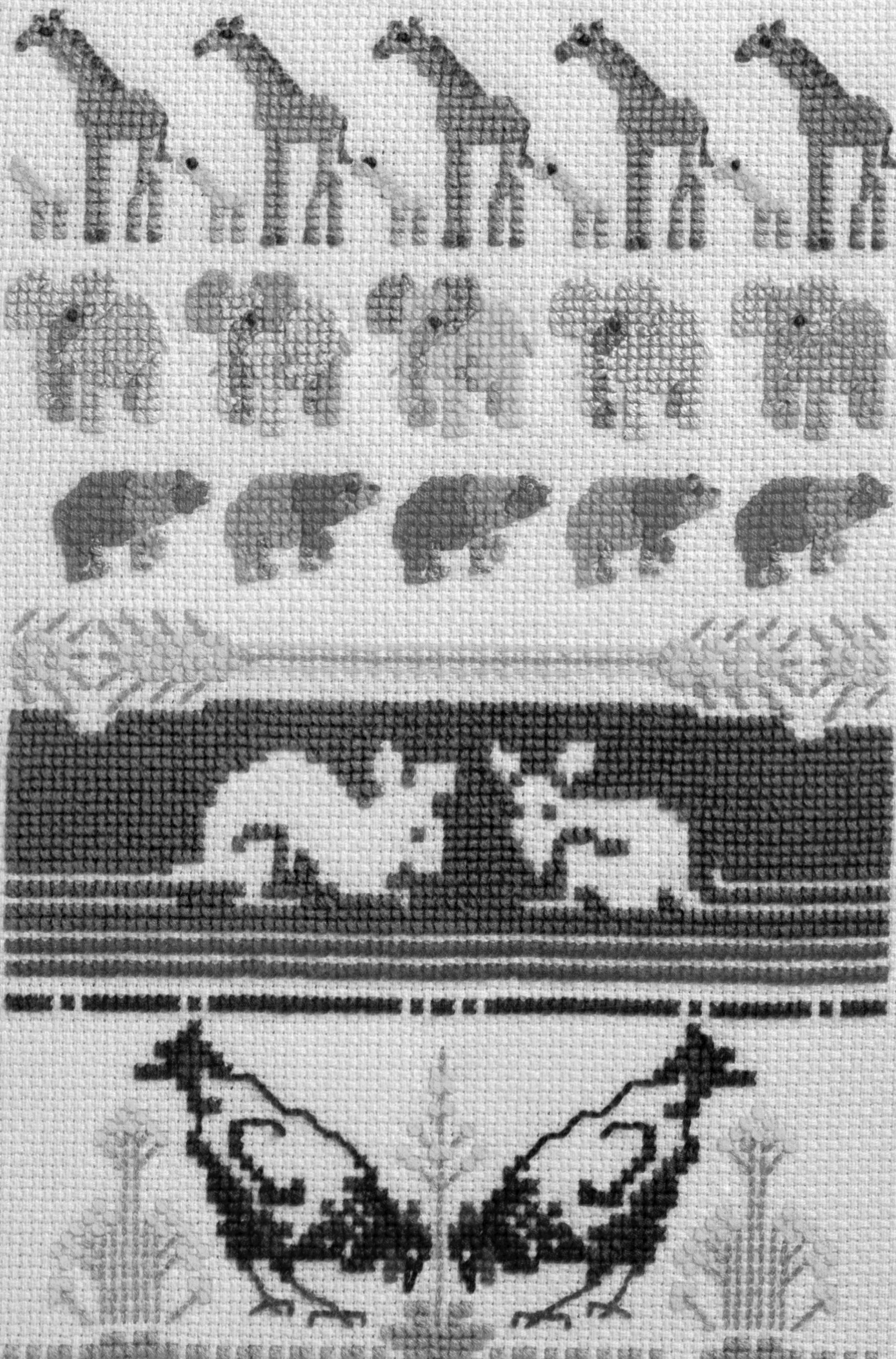

 Instructions on page 94.

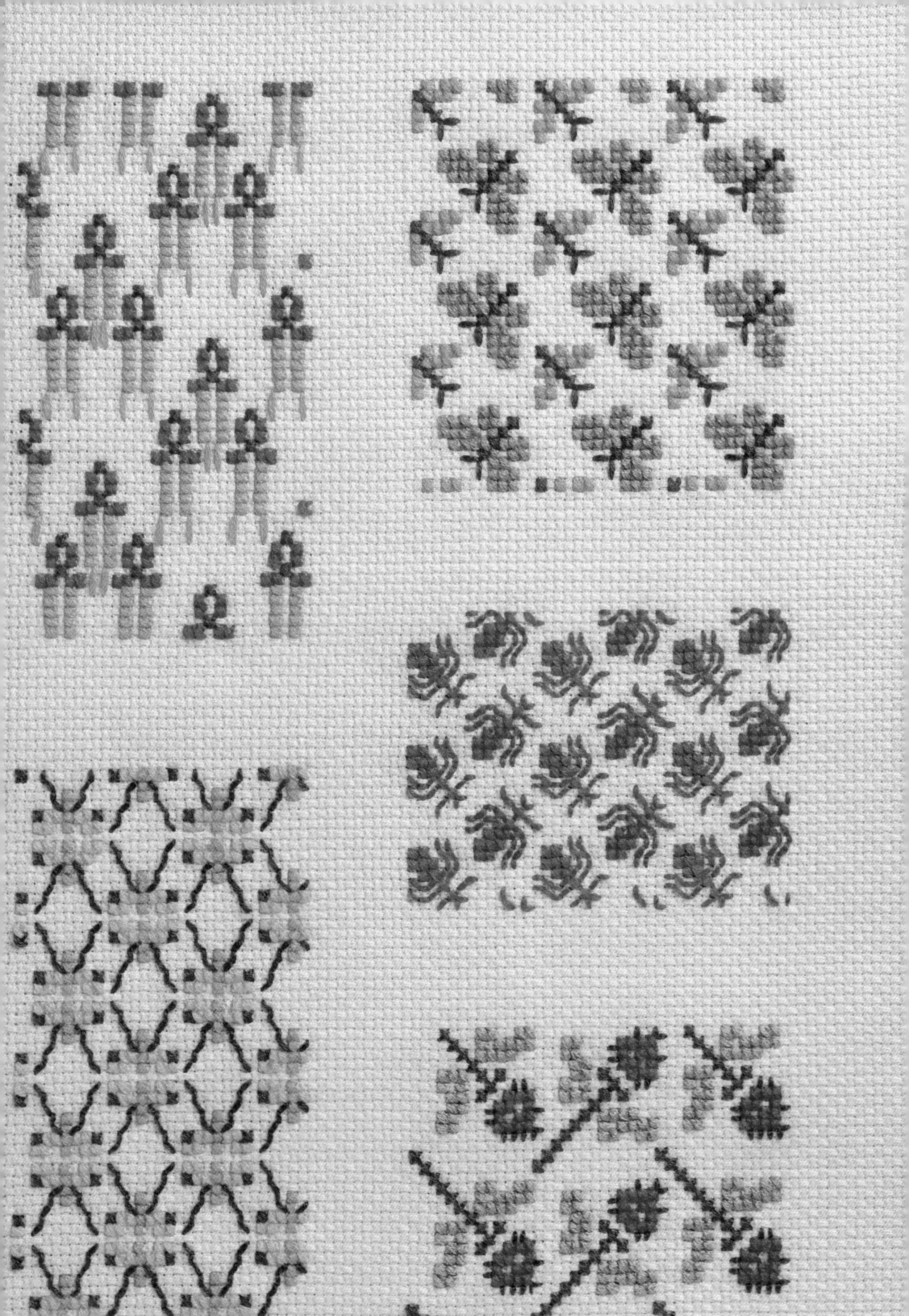

Instructions on page 95.

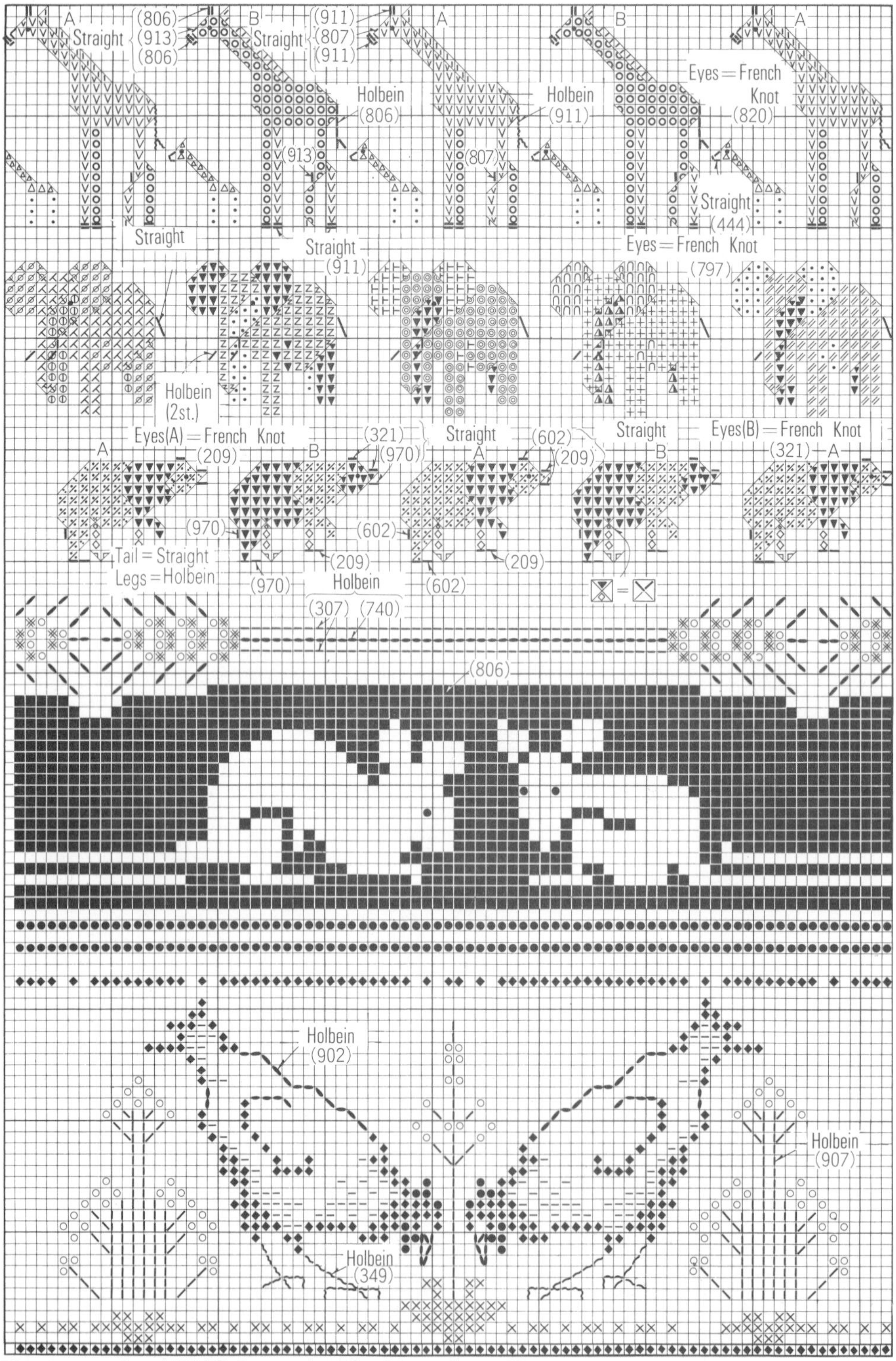

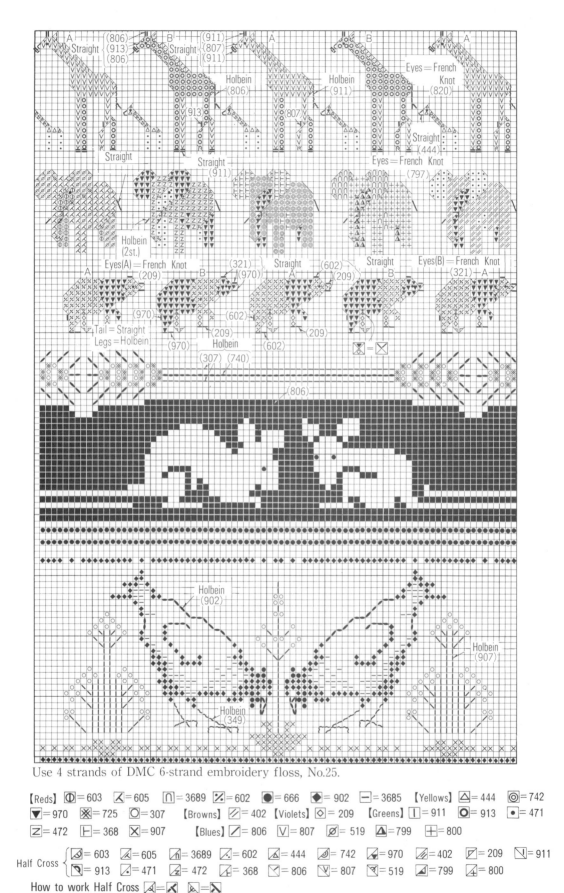

Use 4 strands of DMC 6-strand embroidery floss, No.25.

【Reds】 Φ = 603 ⋌ = 605 ∩ = 3689 ⁒ = 602 ● = 666 ◆ = 902 − = 3685 【Yellows】 △ = 444 ◎ = 742 ▼ = 970 ⋇ = 725 ○ = 307 【Browns】 // = 402 【Violets】 ◇ = 209 【Greens】 I = 911 **O** = 913 • = 471 Z = 472 ⊢ = 368 ✕ = 907 【Blues】 / = 806 V = 807 ∅ = 519 ▲ = 799 + = 800

Half Cross { ∅ = 603 ⋌ = 605 ∩ = 3689 ⁒ = 602 △ = 444 ◎ = 742 ▼ = 970 // = 402 ◇ = 209 I = 911 O = 913 • = 471 Z = 472 ⊢ = 368 / = 806 V = 807 ∅ = 519 ▲ = 799 + = 800 }

How to work Half Cross

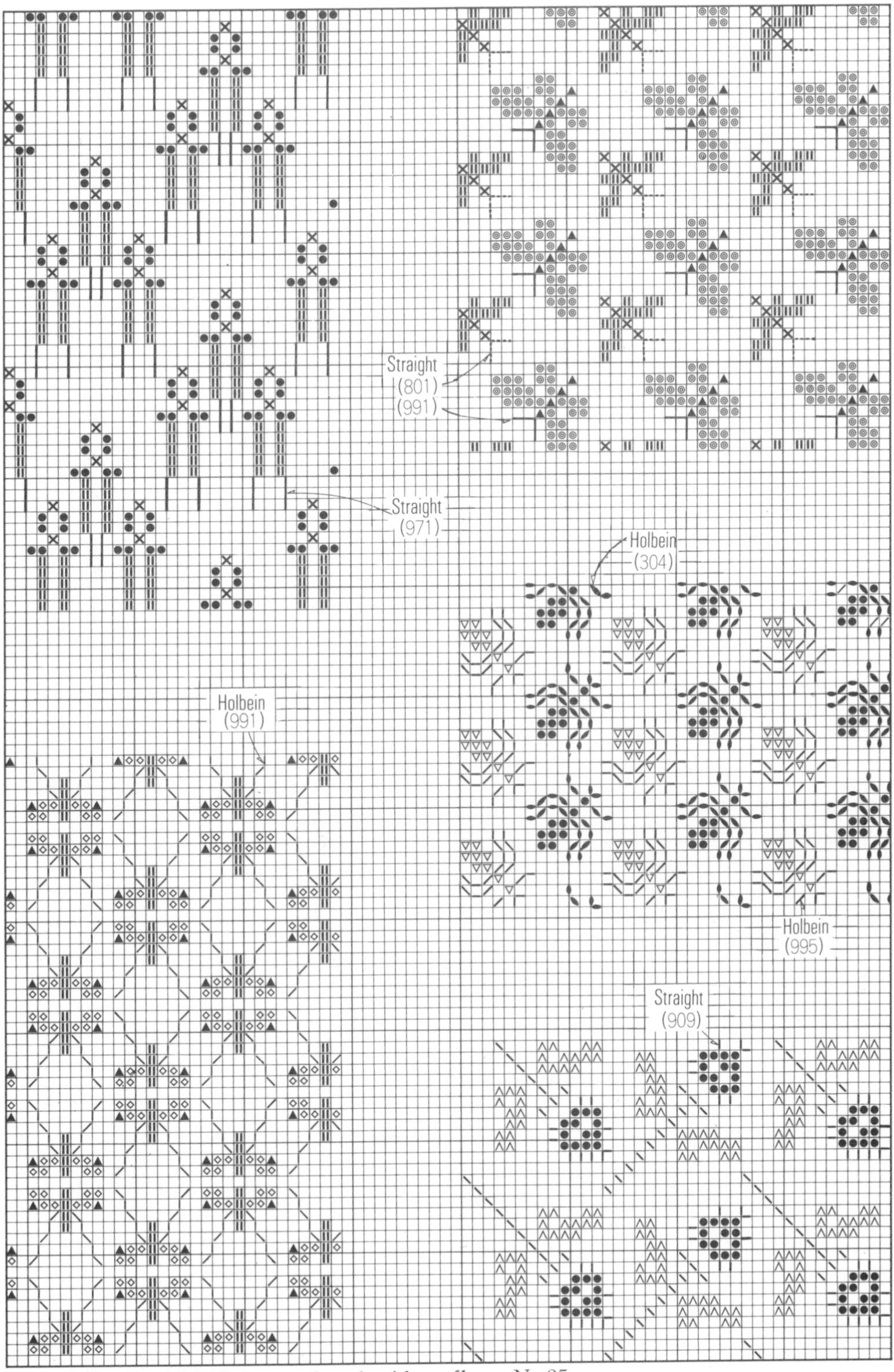

Use 4 strands of DMC 6-strand embroidery floss, No.25.

【Red】 ●=304 【Yellows】 ‖=971 ◇=972 【Brown】 ✕=801 【Greens】 ▼=991 ▽=907
╲=909 【Blues】 △=995 ◎=807

Alphabet

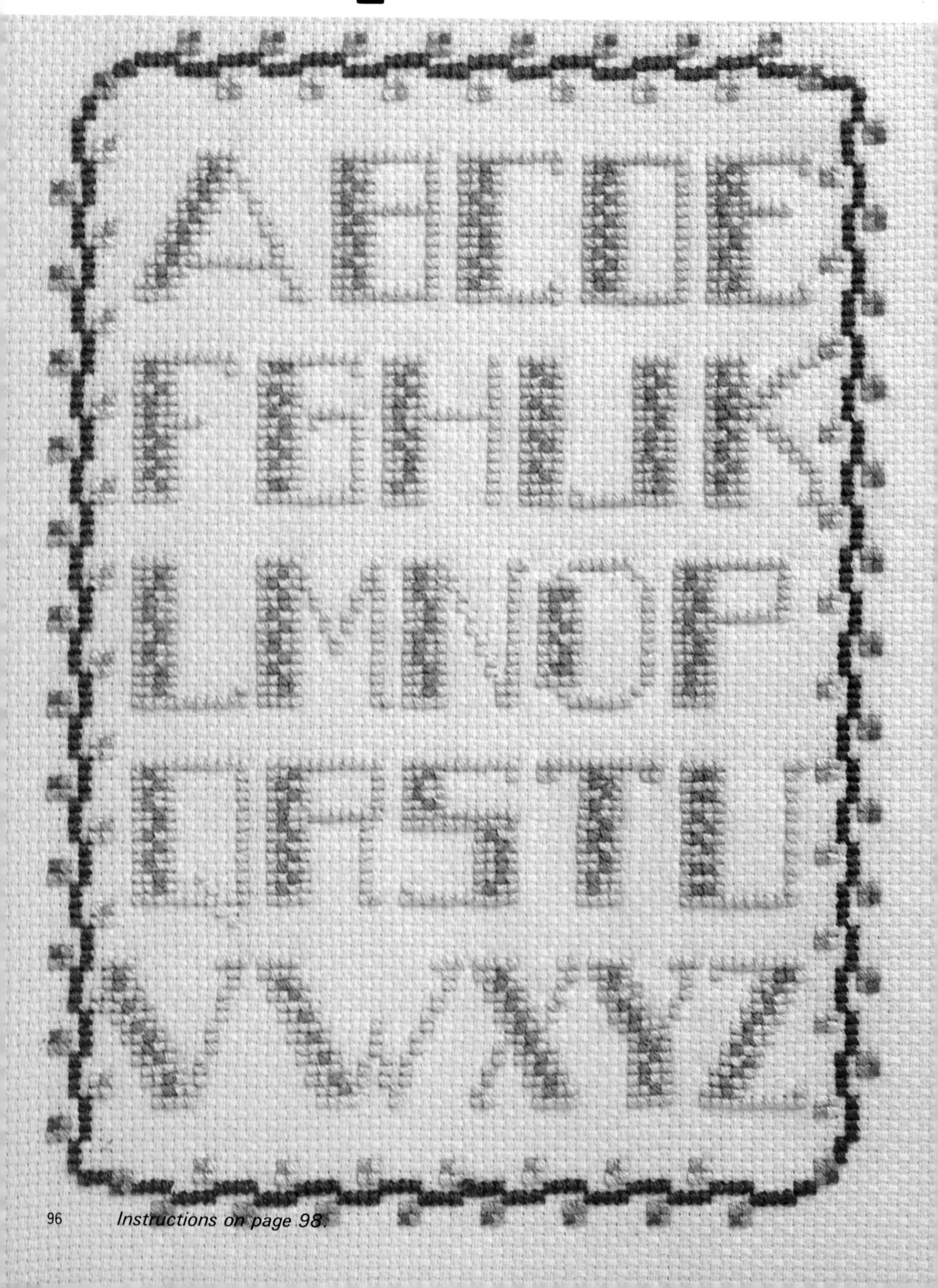

 Instructions on page 98.

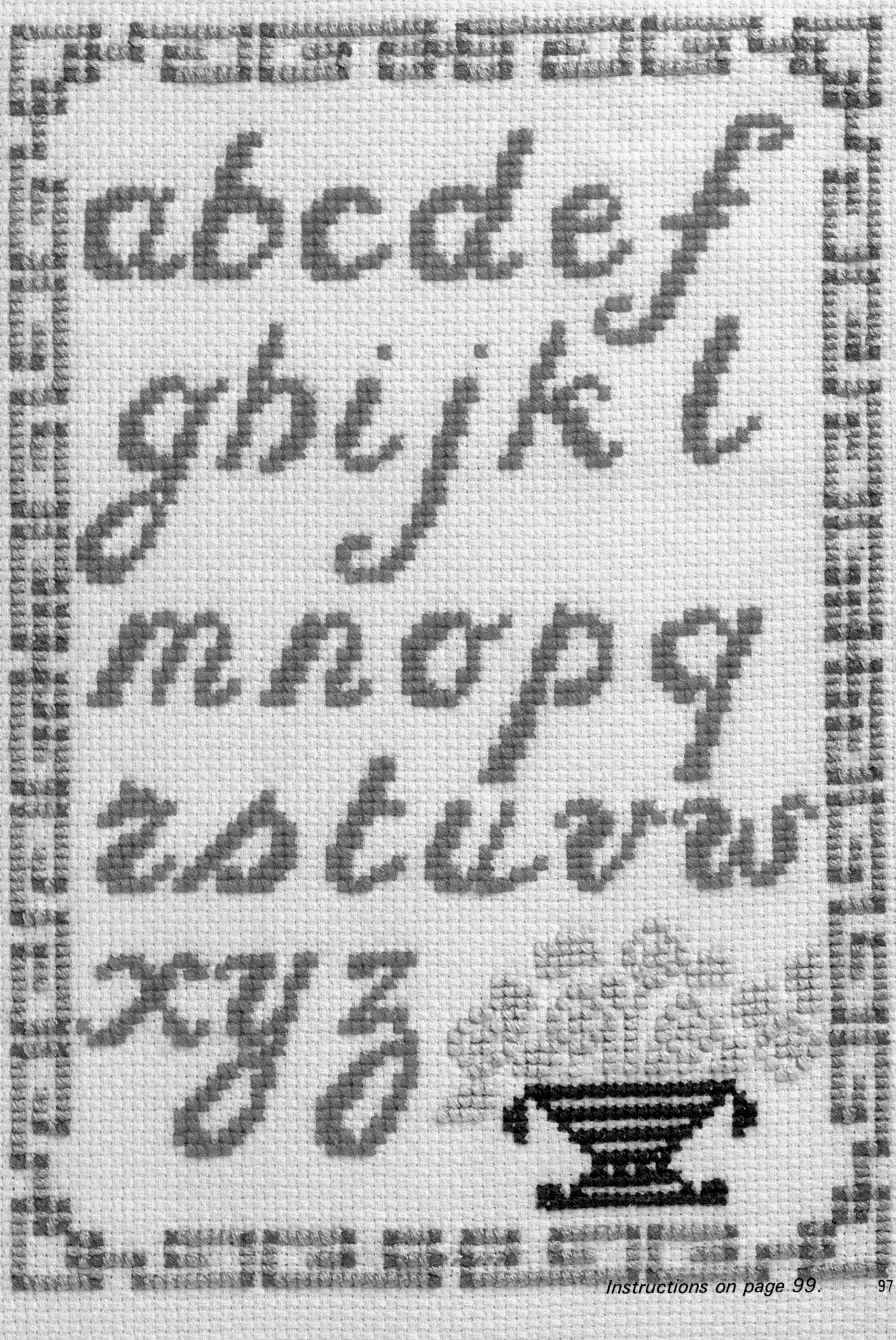

Instructions on page 99.

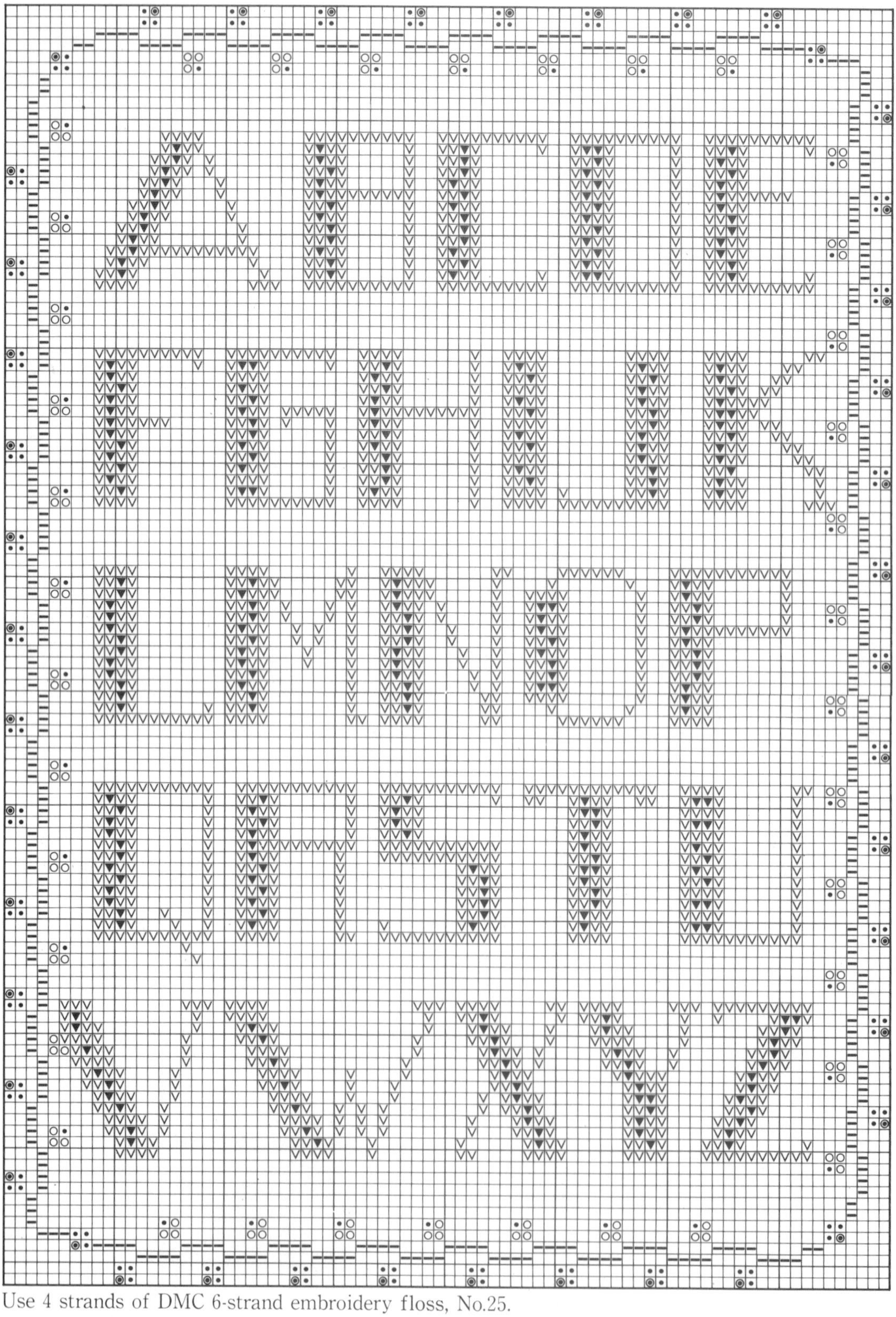

Use 4 strands of DMC 6-strand embroidery floss, No.25.

【Reds】 ◉=606 ○=776 •=899 ▬=3685 【Greens】 ▼=992 V=955

Use 4 strands of DMC 6-strand embroidery floss, No.25.

【Reds】 ●=602 ○=776 【Violets】 ◆=208 ◇=210 【Green】 ☒=472 【Blue】 Ⅱ=820

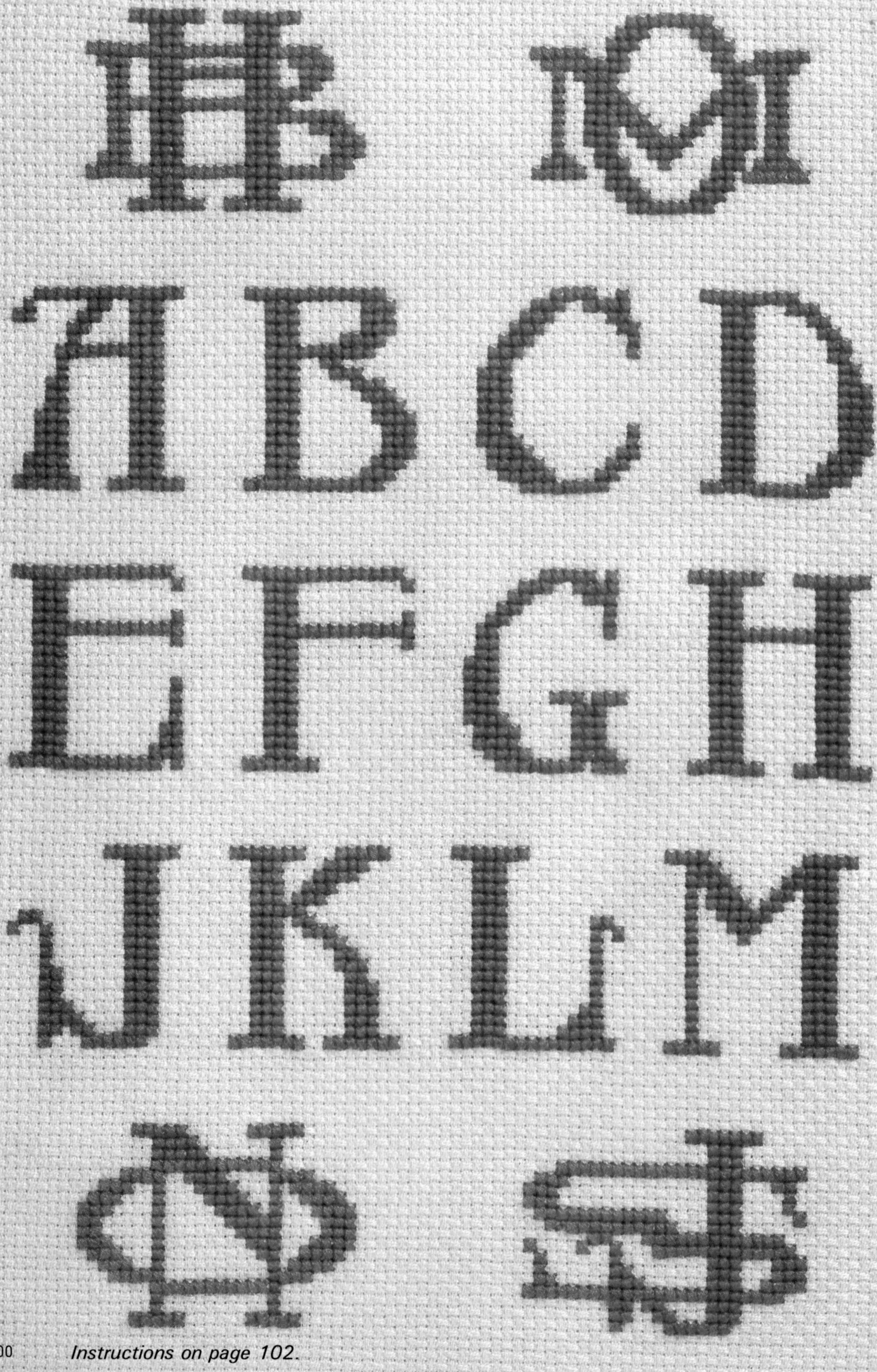

 Instructions on page 102.

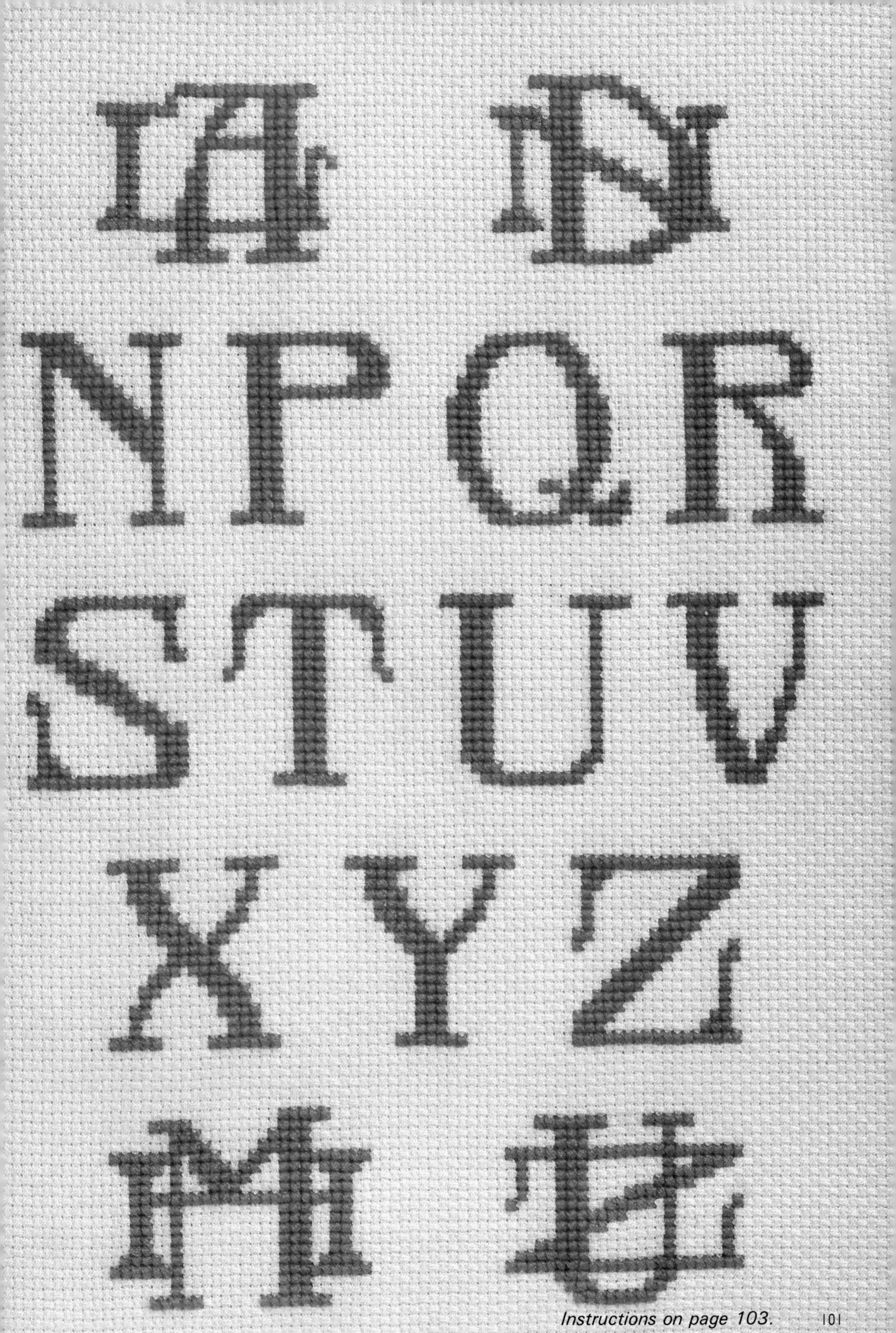

Instructions on page 103.

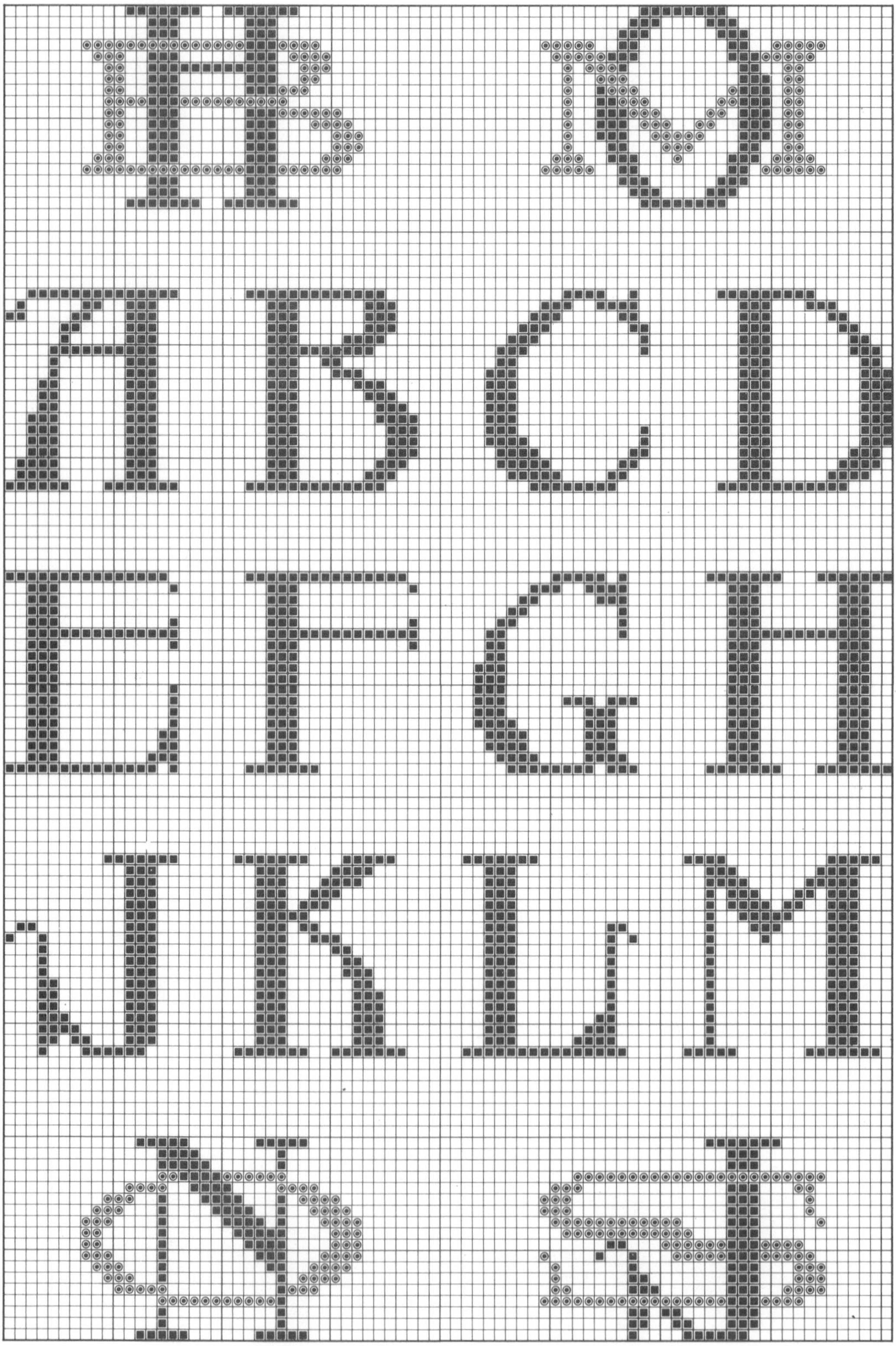

Use 4 strands of DMC 6-strand embroidery floss, No.25.

【Red】 ■=326 【Violet】 ◉=917

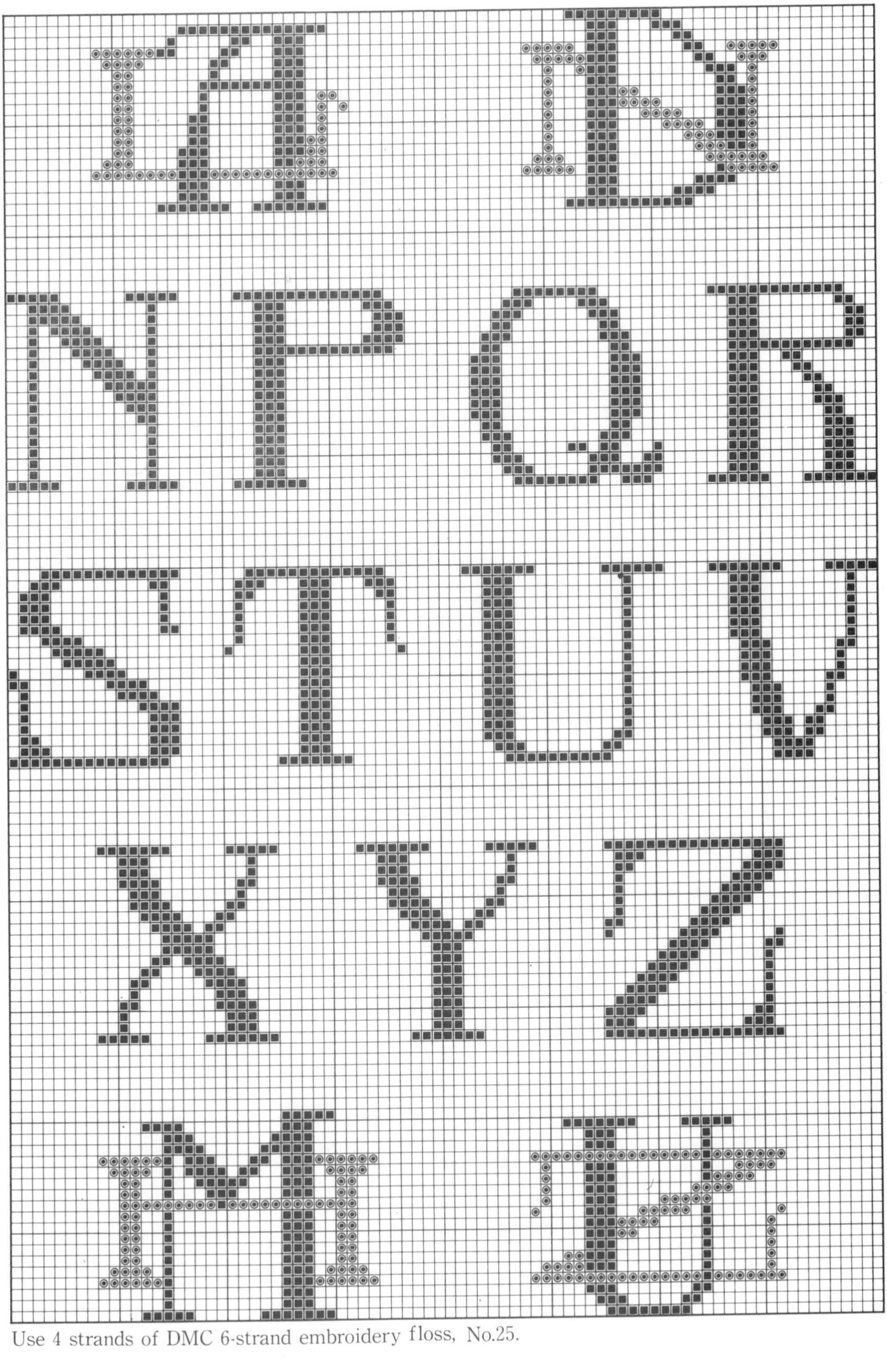

Use 4 strands of DMC 6-strand embroidery floss, No.25.

【Red】 ■=326 【Violet】 ◉=917

 Instructions on page 106.

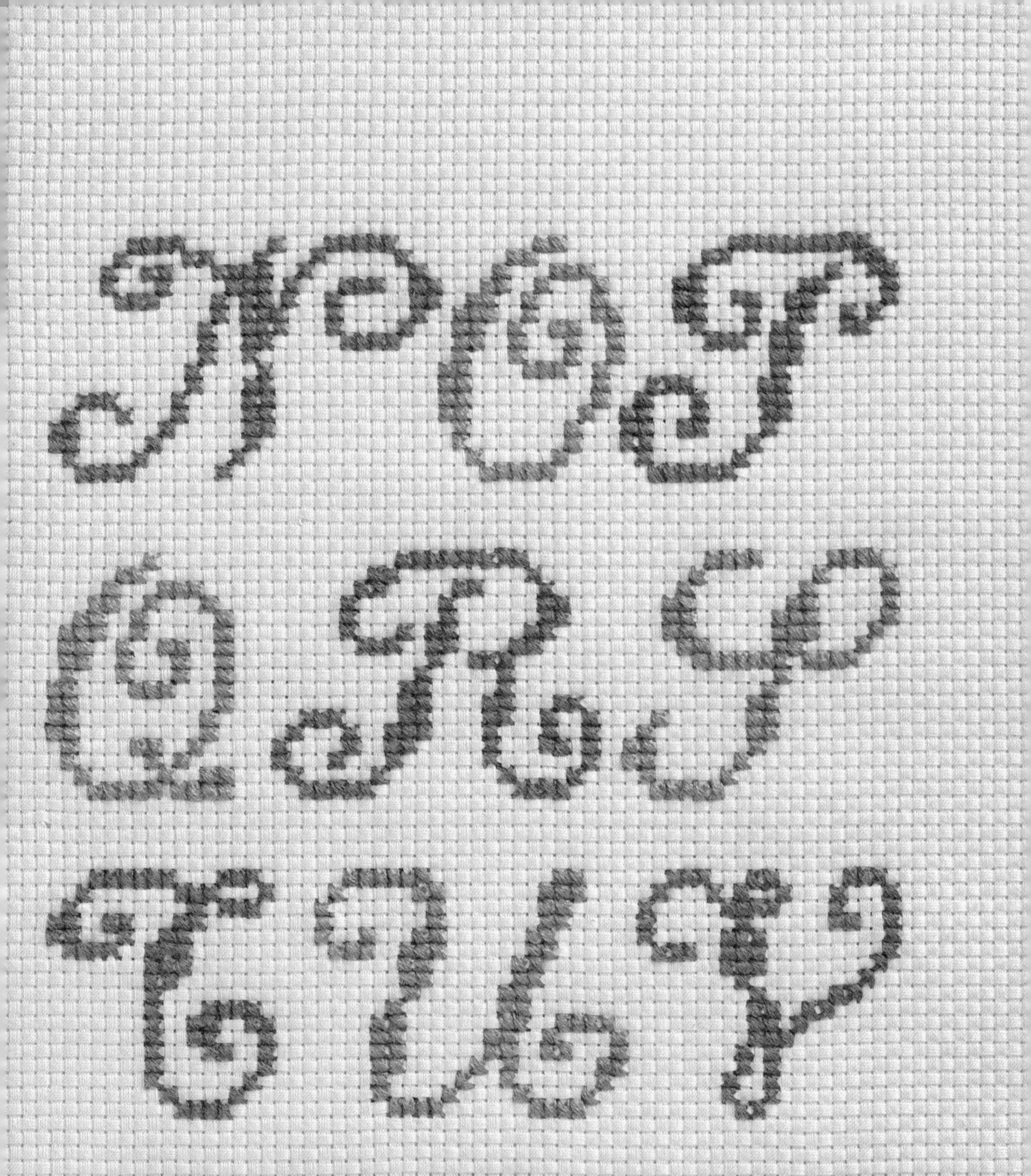

Instructions on page 107.

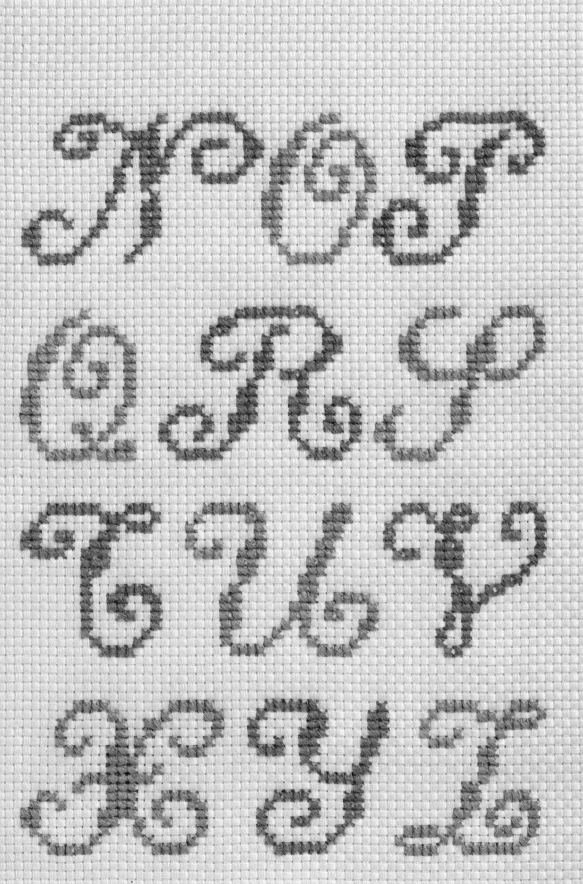

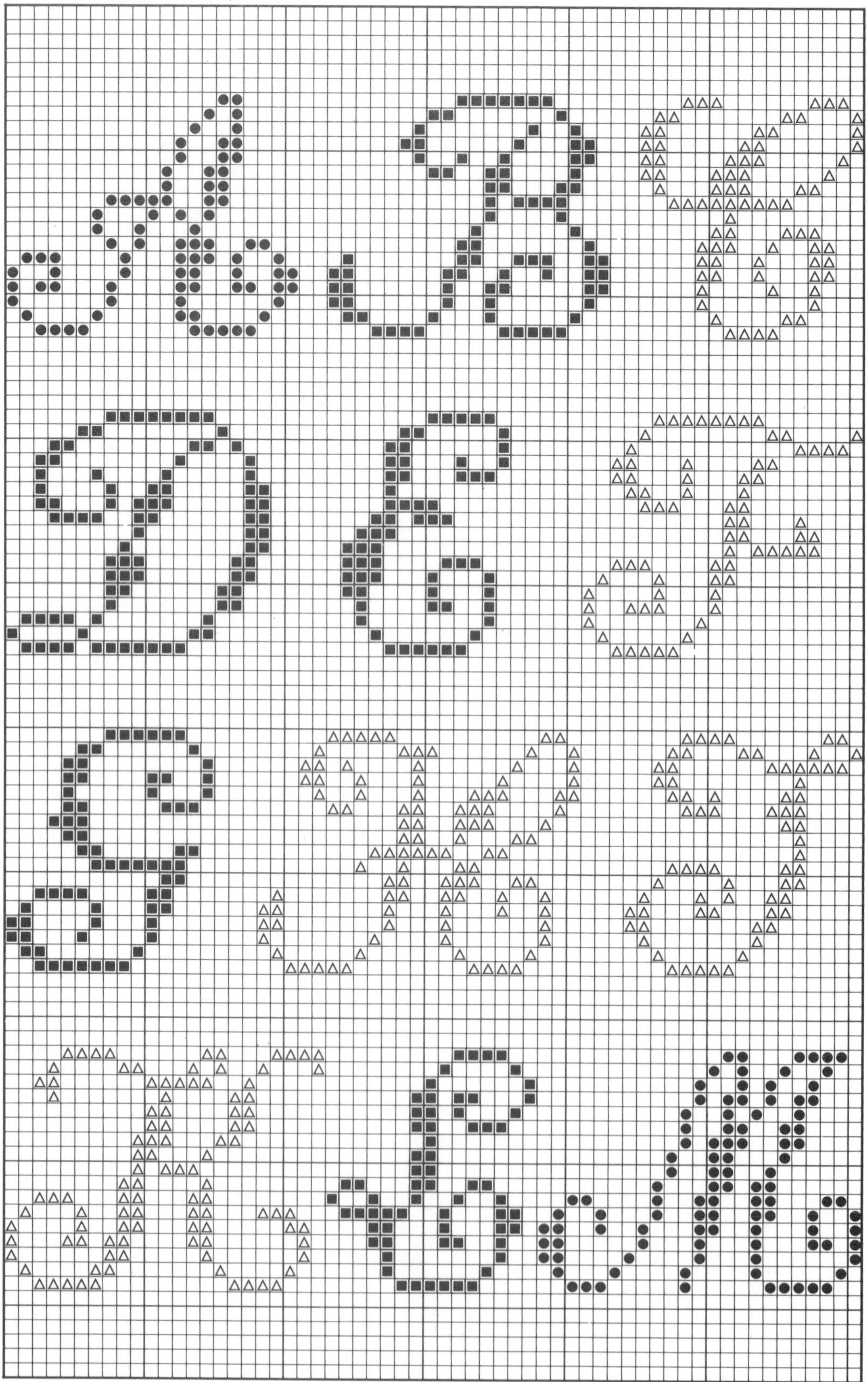

Use 5 strands of DMC 6-strand embroidery floss, No.25.

【Reds】 ● = 326 ■ = 817 △ = 776

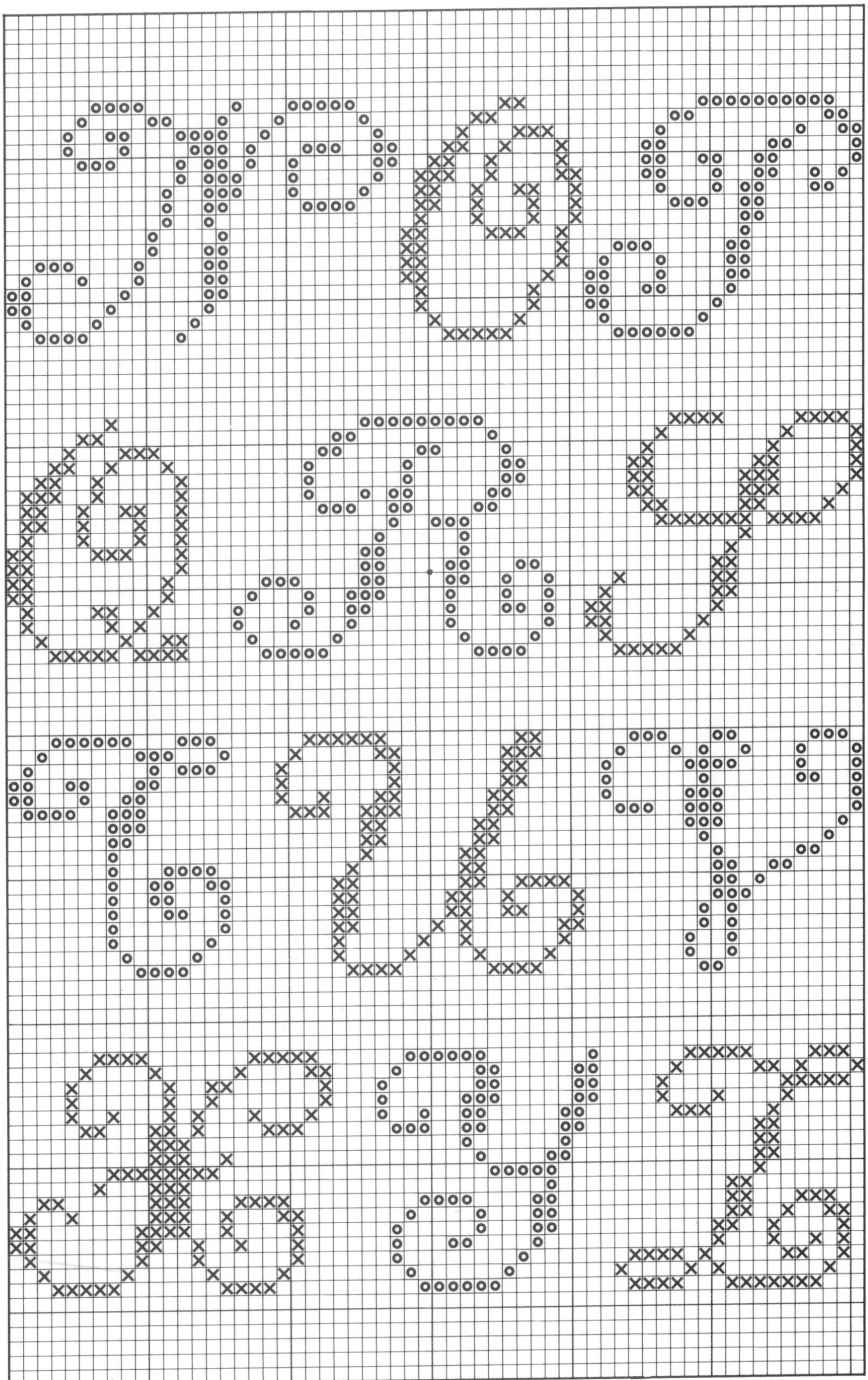

Use 5 strands of DMC 6-strand embroidery floss, No.25.

【Green】 ⊙=701 【Blue】 ☒=518

 Instructions on page 110.

Instructions on page 111.

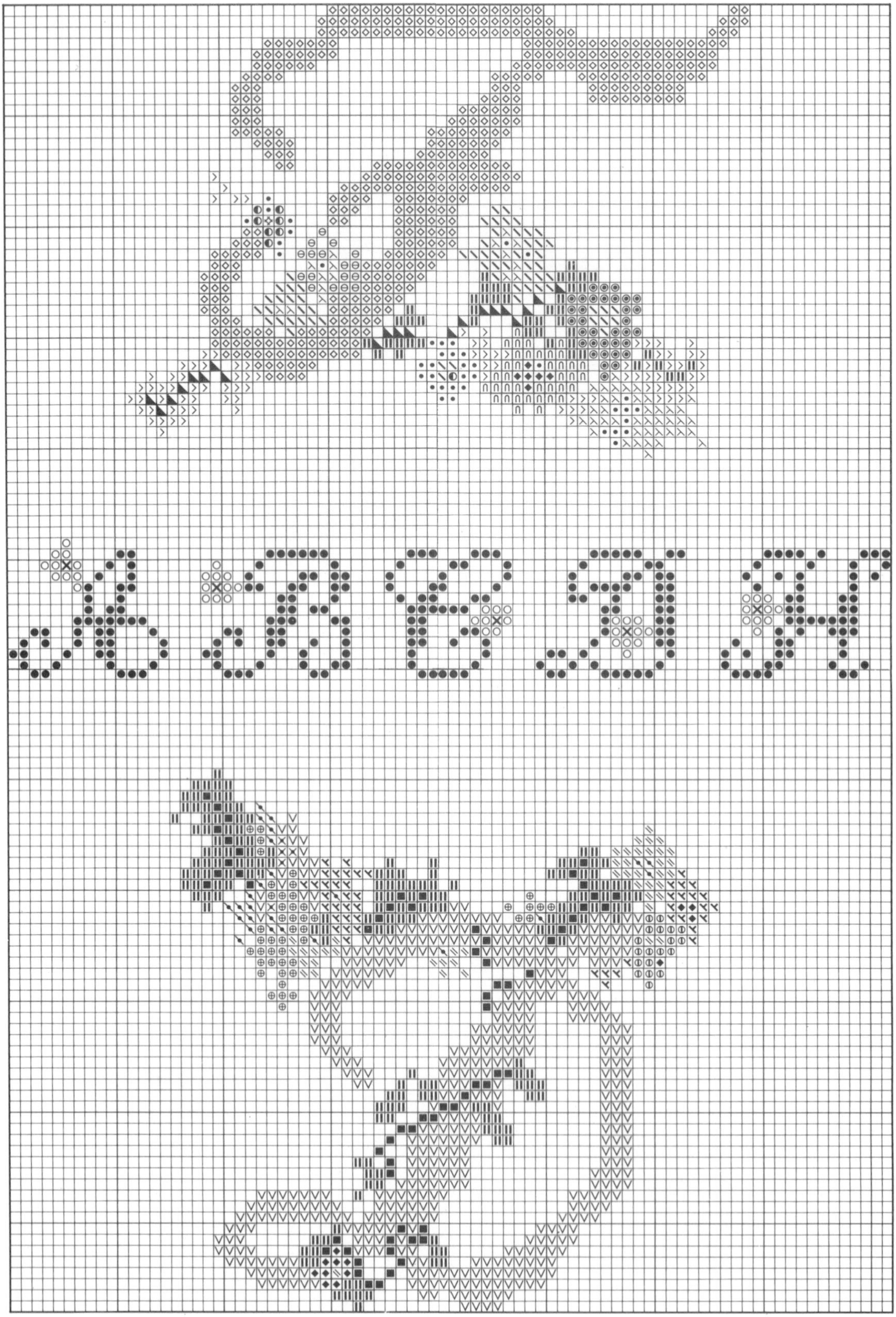

Use 4 strands of DMC 6-strand embroidery floss, No.25.

Common to p.p.110-111. 【Reds】 • =309 ⋋ =335 ◐ =608 ⊖ =818 ● =347 ○ =3689 ↘ =600 ⊕ =603 Φ =606 ⑊ =894 ✕ =947 【Yellows】 ╲ =741 + =307 ◎ =740 【Violets】 ∩ =210 ◆ =552

【Greens】 ◇=368 ◣=890 ‖=906 >=3013 ✕=966 ■=935 △=993 【Blues】 ◉=312 ✧=813

⊠=809 V=827

 Instructions on page 3.

Basics in Cross-Stitch

Cross-Stitch

In Cross-Stitch, the design is worked regularly by making crosses in the same direction. Use the even-weave fabrics or canvas which you can count the threads easily. You may use a checked fabric like gingham as a guide for Cross-Stitch. Use a blunt needle made for Cross-Stitch with which you can pick up the threads easily. You may use a blunt tapestry needle when working on heavyweight fabrics, wool or knit.

To work horizontally:

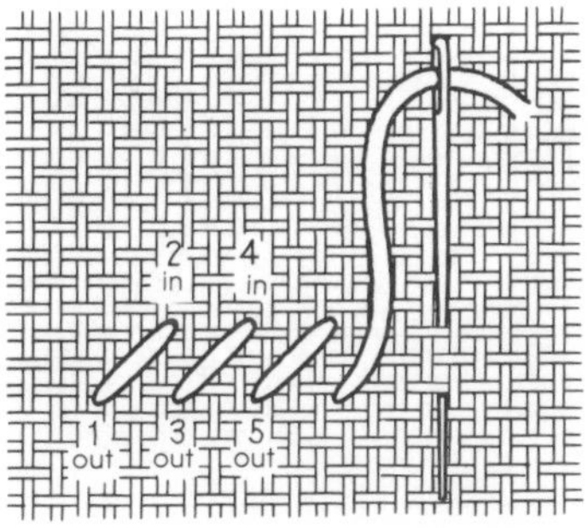

Work across all stitches in each row from left to right.

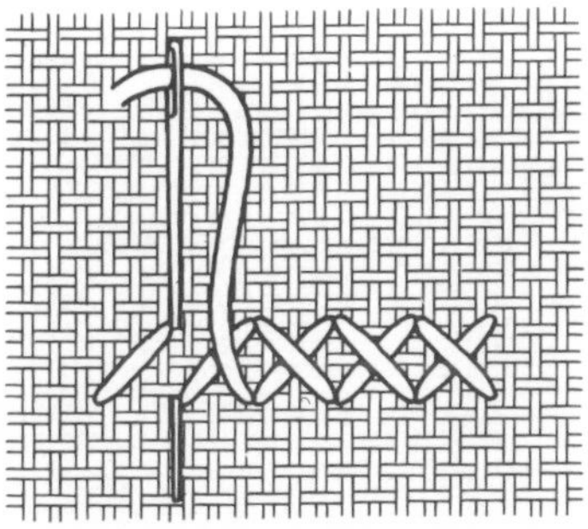

When coming to the end, cross back in the other direction from right to left.

To work downward horizontally:

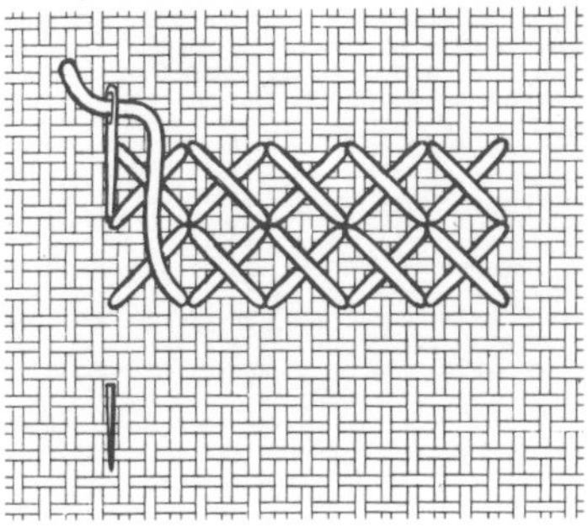

To work upward horizontally:

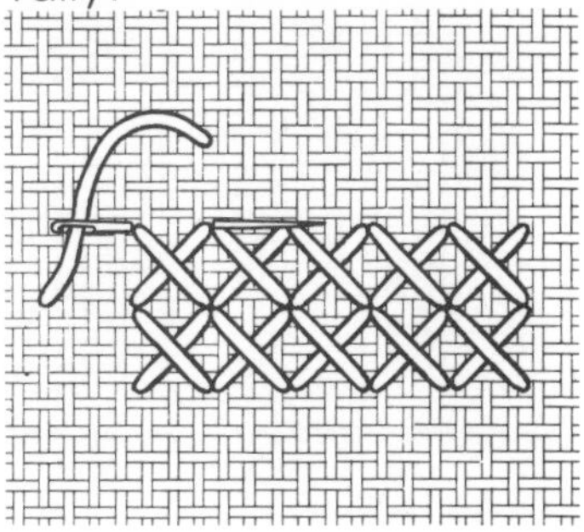

To complete each cross horizontally:

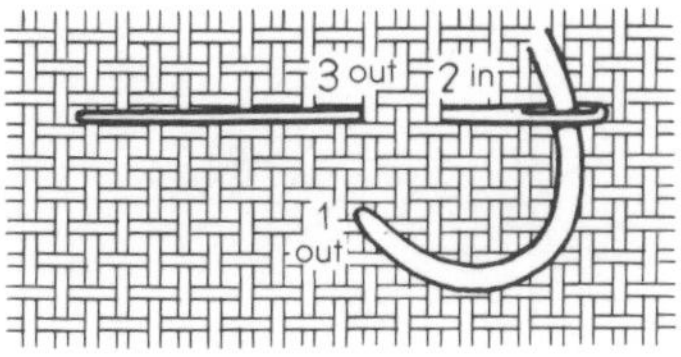

Bring the thread out at the lower left and take a stitch from 2 to 3.

Insert the needle at 4 and take a stitch to 5.

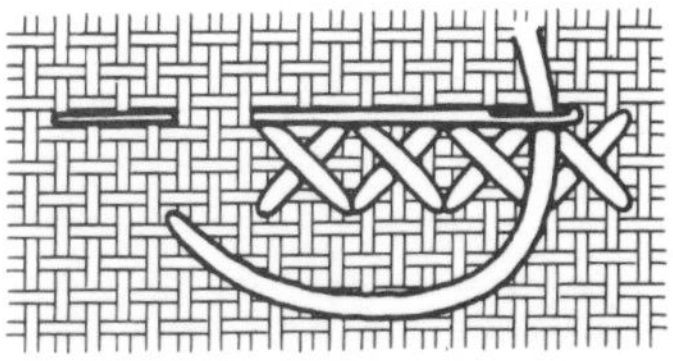

Continue to work, completing each cross.

To complete each cross vertically:

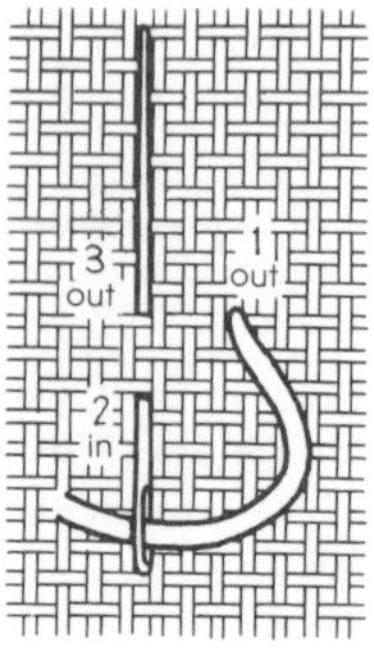

Bring the thread out at the upper right and take a stitch from 2 to 3.

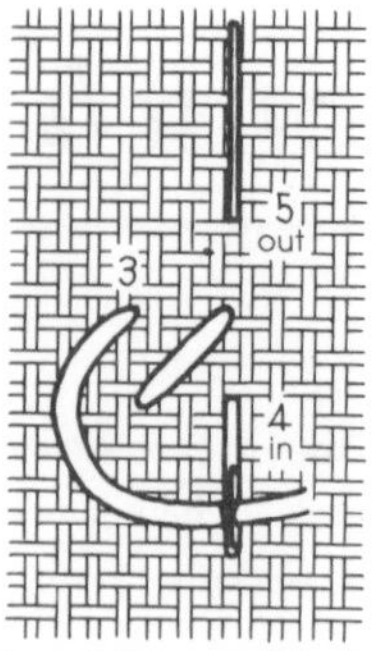

Insert the needle at 4 to form a cross and take a stitch to 5.

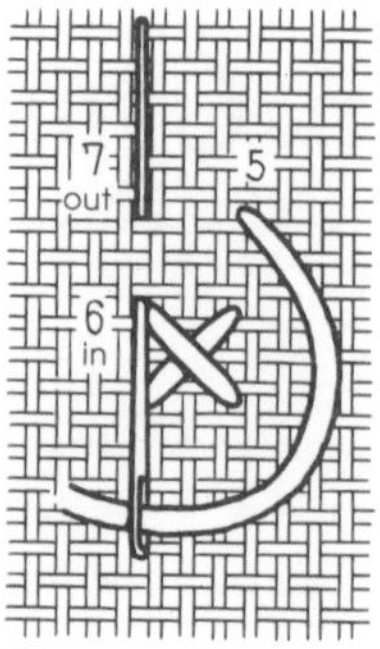

Take a stitch from 6 to 7.

Complete each cross working vertically. The direction of the threads must be the same, when working downward or upward.

To work upward diagonally:

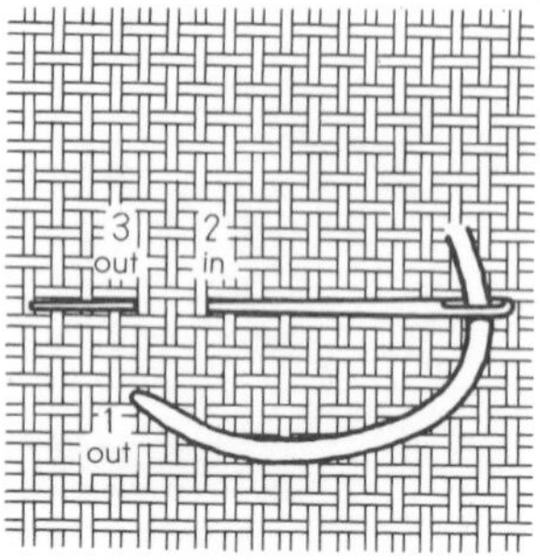

Bring the thread out at 1 and take a horizontal stitch from 2 to 3.

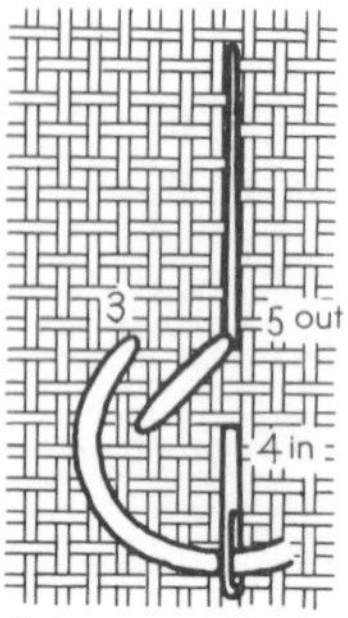

Take a vertical stitch from 4 to 5.

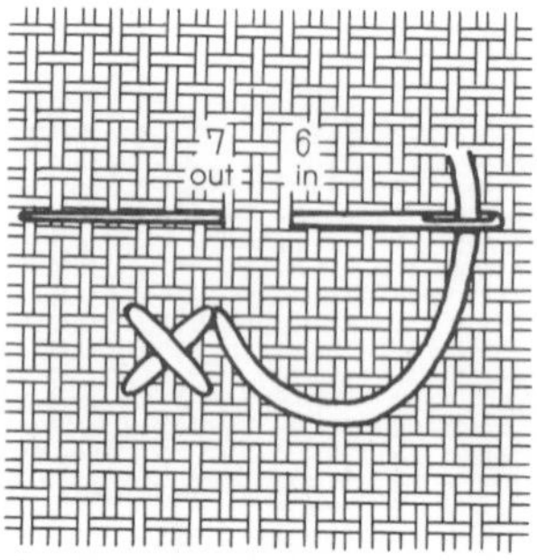

Continue to work upward diagonally, completing each cross.

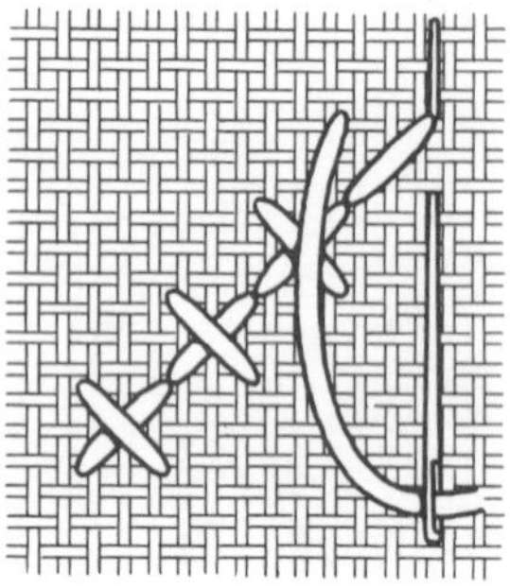

To work downward diagonally:

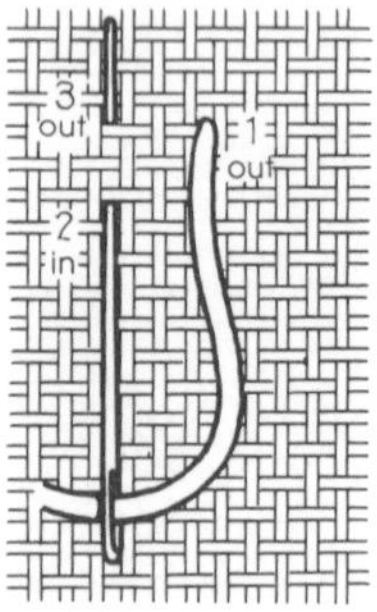

Bring the thread out at 1 and take a vertical stitch from 2 to 3.

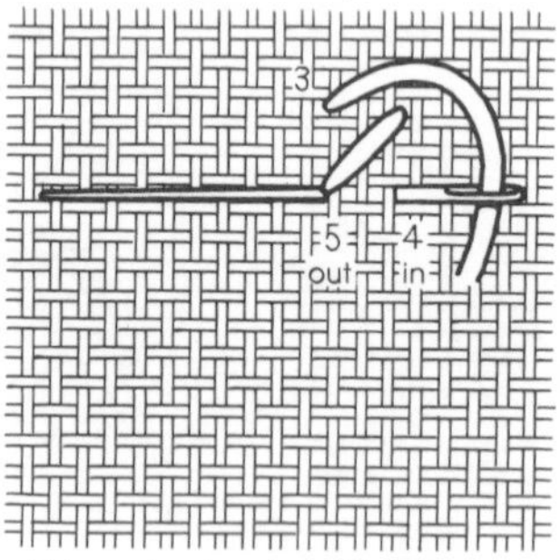

Take a horizontal stitch from 4 to 5.

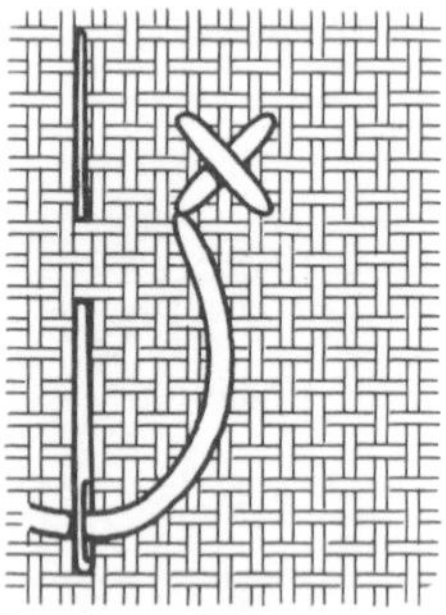

Continue to work downward diagonally, completing each cross.

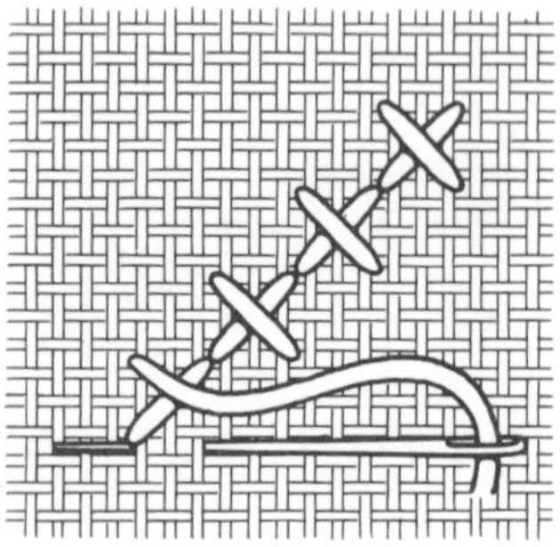

Overcast the cut-edge before you work.

Suitable fabrics for Cross Stitch are easy to fray. Overcast the cut-edge before you start working for easy handling.

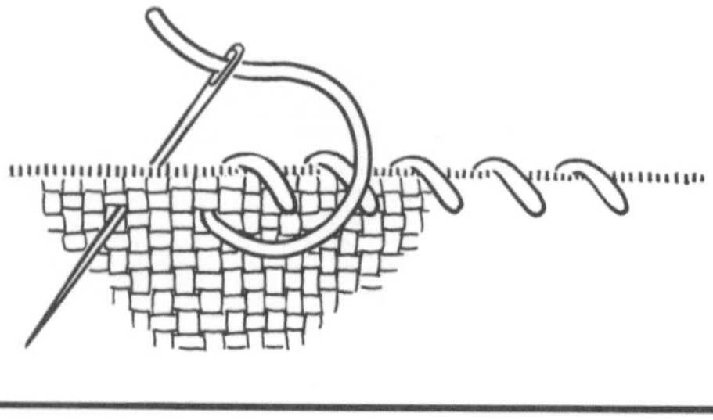

Holbein Stitch

This is also called Line Stitch and is sometimes used for outlining or dividing cross-stitched area.

The stitch is completed by running stitches in both ways. Stitches on the wrong side are the same on the front.

Straight Line:

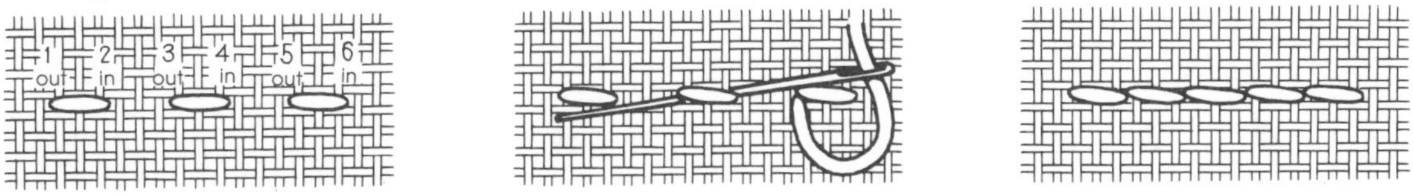

Take stitches of equal length.

When coming to the end of design, return in the same way filling in the spaces left by the first row. Always insert the needle in the same direction for a neater finish.

Diagonal Line:

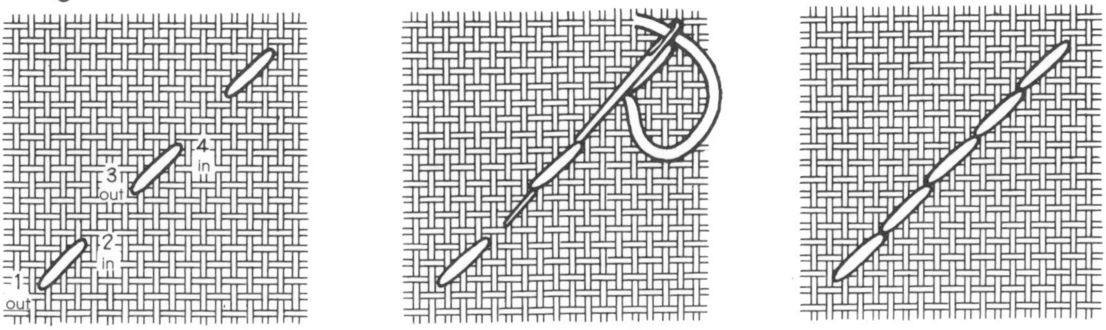

Take stitches of equal length diagonally.

When coming to the end of design, return in the same way as for the Straight Line.

Zigzag Line:

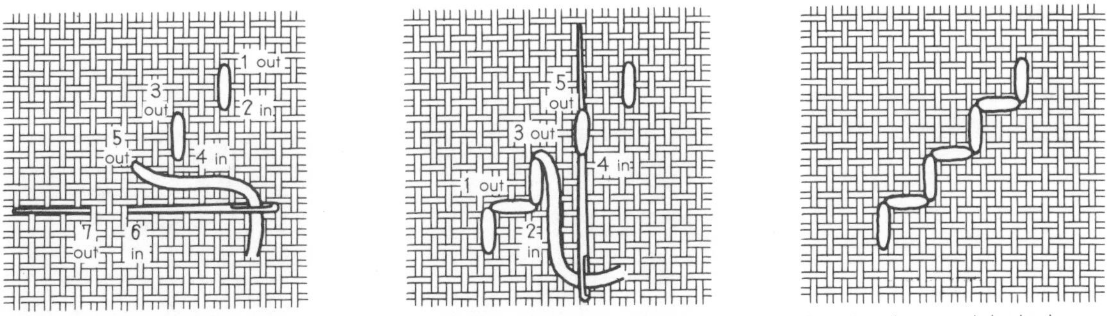

Take vertical stitches from upper right.

Bring the thread at 1 and take a vertical stitch from 2 to 3.

On return journey, take horizontal stitches to make zigzag line.

Double Cross-Stitch

Work Cross-Stitch first. Then work another Cross-Stitch over the previous one. Always bring the needle out and insert it in the same way.

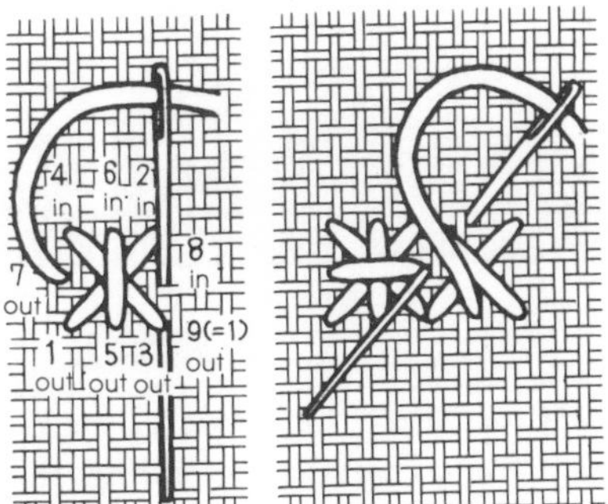

Half Cross-Stitch

One half of the cross or a diagonal stitch is usually called Half Cross-Stitch, but the stitches shown below are called Half Cross-Stitch in this book. The directions of the stitches are shown as follows.

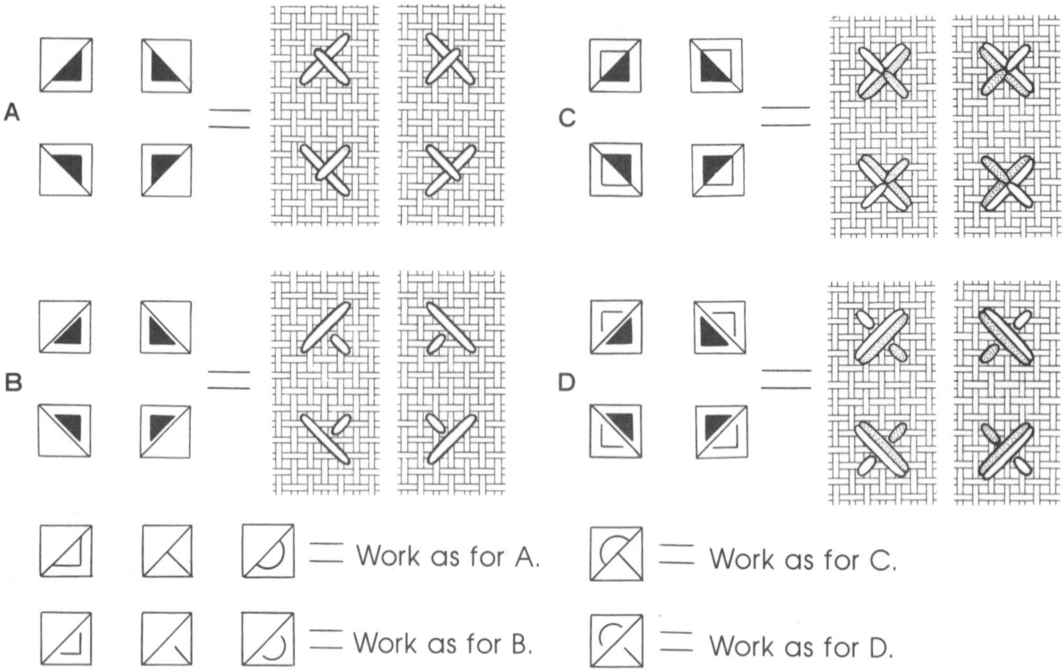

Fabrics, Threads and Needles

Fabrics

Aida cloth

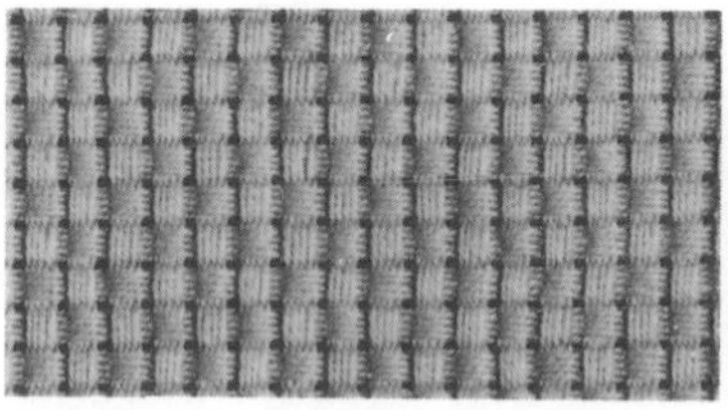
Java canvas (35 threads per 10 cm)

Java canvas (25 threads per 10 cm)

Even-weave linen

Oxford cloth

Davosa canvas

In the Cross-Stitch Embroidery, the designs are worked from charts by counting the threads of the fabric. Use even-weave fabric or canvas whose threads can be counted easily.

The fabrics suited to the Cross-Stitch Embroidery are shown in the photos on the opposite page. Most of them are cotton or linen, but wool, silk or synthetics may be also used depending on its purpose.
Aida cloth and Java canvas ... Are even-weave fabrics and the most suitable for the Cross-Stitch Embroidery.
Davosa canvas ... Is woven with single thick thread, thus this is a heavy-weight canvas. This is often used for the Cross-Stitch Embroidery and the Free-style Embroidery with bold designs.
Oxford cloth ... Is often used for the Counted Treade Embroidery as well as Aida cloth. This is evenly woven with double threads.
Even-weave linen ... Light or medium-weight linen is mostly used. Light-weight linen is suitable for making tablecloths with complicated designs.

Counted Thread Embroidery

In the Cross-Stitch Embroidery, the finished size will vary depending on fineness or coarseness of the fabric used. Always check the thread count per inch when buying the fabric.

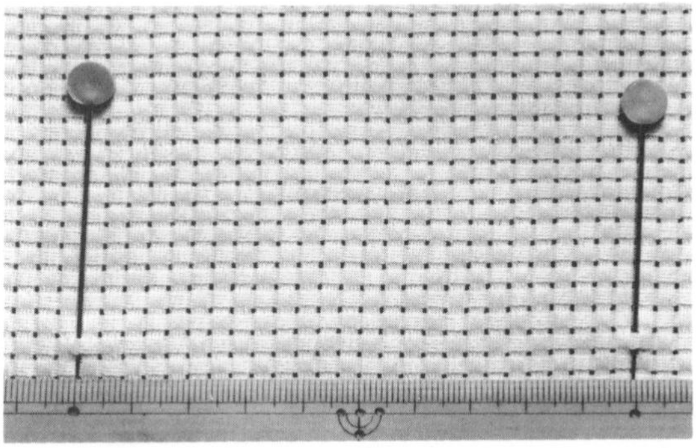

Threads

A wide variety of threads is available in the market, but choose the most suitable thread for the purpose, the design and the fabric.
Six Strand Floss, No. 25 – One thread consists of 6 strands, and measures 8m per skein. You can pull out as many threads as required from the bundle if necessary (according to the design).
Pearl Cotton, No. 5 – Single thick thread, and is quite lustrous. One skein measures 25m. Suitable for rough stitches.
Cotton à broder, No. 4 – Made of four two-ply threads twisted together.
Besides these, you have a wide variety of them such as cottons, rayons, silk, wools ... even metal threads. The sizes also range from thick, medium, fine and extreme fine.

Needles

Blunt-pointed needles or tapestry needles are often used for the Counted Thread Embroidery. The needles from No. 19 to No. 23 are suitable for the Cross-Stitch Embroidery. The larger the number, the finer and shorter the needle.

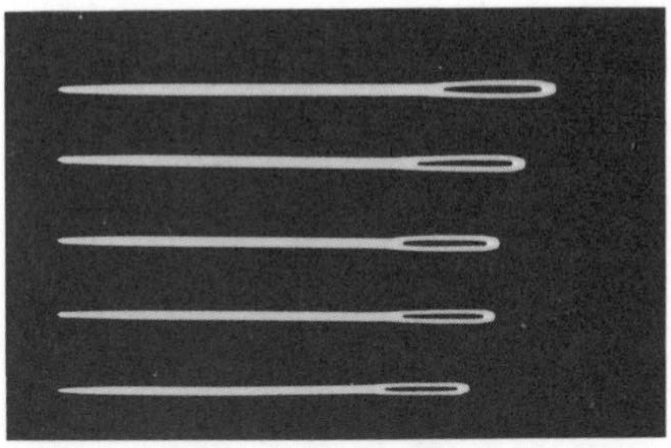

Effective Combination of Fabric and Thread

The chart on the right shows the effective combination of the fabric and the embroidery thread. If the background fabric is shown through the embroidery or if you have a tendency to pull the working thread too tightly, use more strands of the thread in needle.

Fabrics	Gauge (10 cm)	Six strand fross, No. 25
Aida cloth	44 threads	3 – 4 strands
Java canvas (Medium weight)	35 threads	6 strands
Java canvas (Heavy weight)	25 threads	10 – 12 strands
Davosa canvas	71 threads	6 strands
Oxford cloth	80 threads	4 strands

How to handle thread

The threads Nos. 25, 5 and 4 come in a bundle or ring, depending on the manufacturer. When they are formed in a ring, untie the twist, and cut one end of the ring with scissors, and pull out one by one. When they are gathered together and held by one or two paper labels, pull out the length from the core of the bundle.

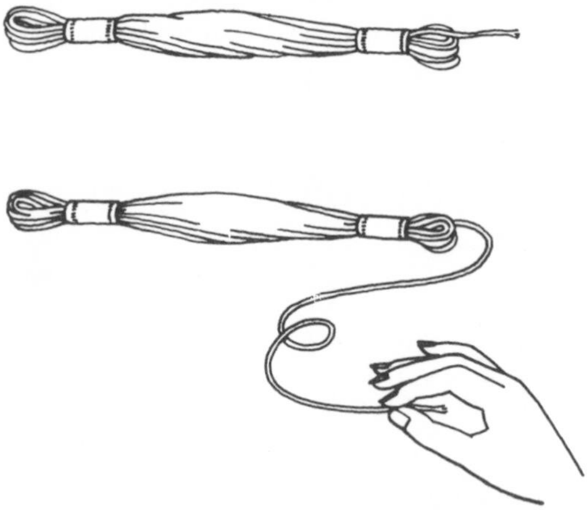

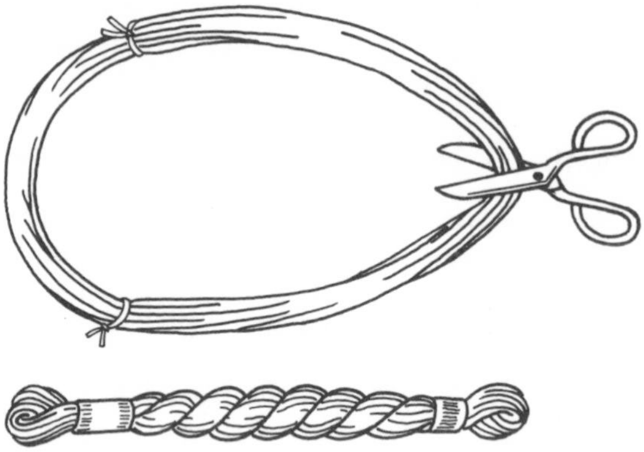

How to pass thread through needle

When you pass 4 strands of the thread through an embroidery needle, fold the ends of the threads, and insert the folded edge through hole of the needle. (See illustration at right) Do the same way when you pass a thick yarn like wool.

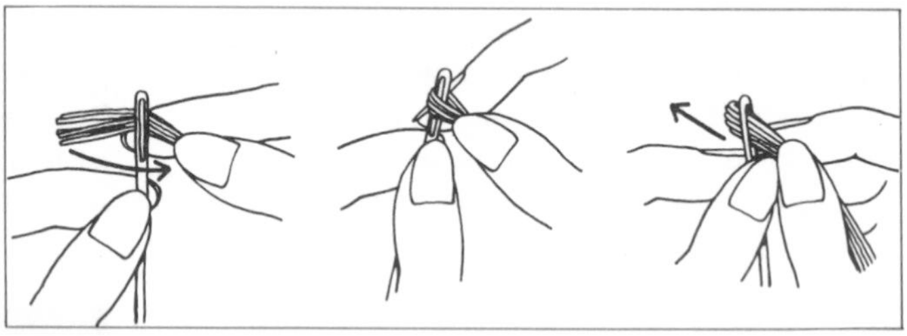

Direction of Stitches

All the crosses of the piece should be in the same direction. Always work all the underneath threads in one direction and the top threads in the opposite.

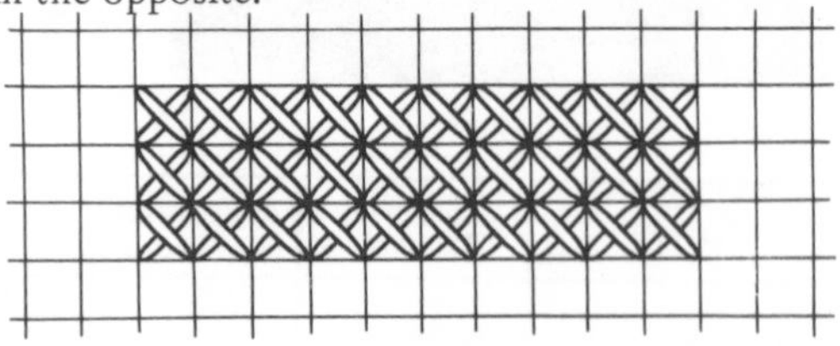

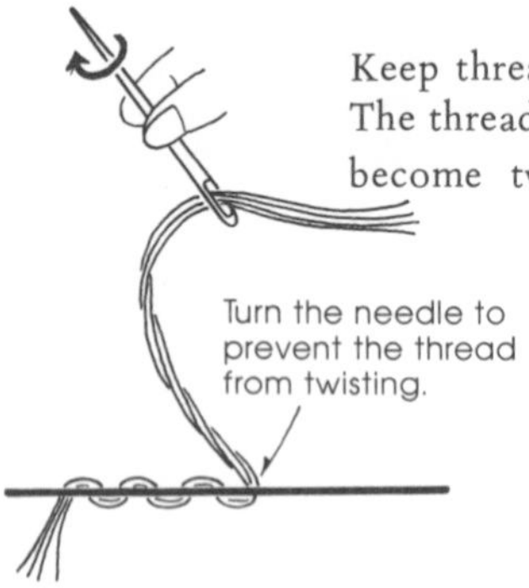
Turn the needle to prevent the thread from twisting.

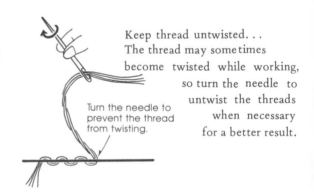

Keep thread untwisted...
The thread may sometimes become twisted while working, so turn the needle to untwist the threads when necessary for a better result.

Length of thread ... Cut the thread about 50cm long at a time. If you use longer thread, the lust of the thread will be lost and you may have a poor result.

Where to start ... You may start wherever you like provided that you count the threads and follow the chart properly. However, it is easier to work when starting at center or at the corner of a motif.

Tension of thread ... Pulling the thread too tightly or too loosely will damage the finished work. Always keep the tension of the thread evenly.

Embroidery hoop ... You may work cross-stitches without using an embroidery hoop, but it will help keeping even tension of the thread. Be sure to use an embroidery hoop for working Half Cross-Stitch.

How to start

Start embroidery leaving the end of the thread twice as long as the needle to be used. When the embroidery is finished, weave both ends of the thread into the stitches on the wrong side. It is advisable not to make knots at the beginning and ending, for they will show on the front or sometimes come out through the fabric. When using double or even number of strands, fold the thread in half and start working as shown at left.

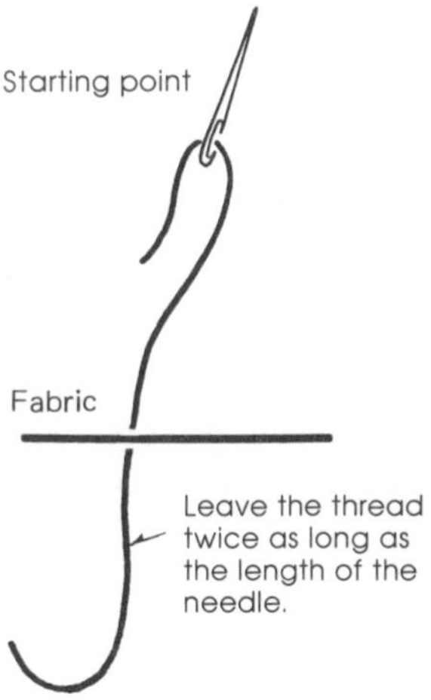

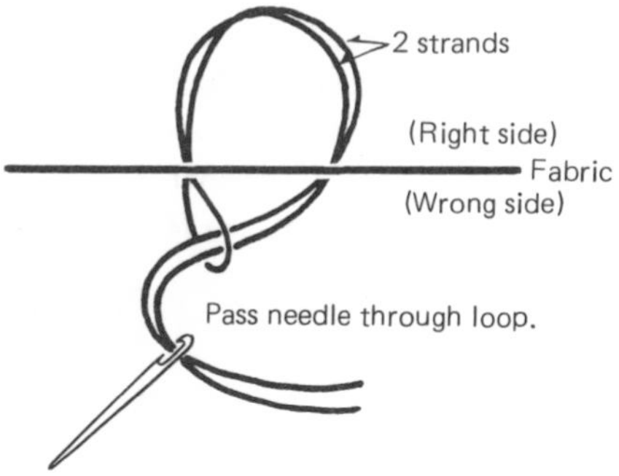

Finishing

Check whether there are any mistakes in the direction of the stitches or any skipped area. Also make sure that the ends of the thread are woven into the stitches and trimmed off neatly.

How to press

Spray water over the wrong side of the embroidered piece. Place a blanket covered with a white cloth on the ironing board. Place the damp embroidered piece on the top with the wrong side up. Press gently stretching the fabric along the grain, then along the selvages.

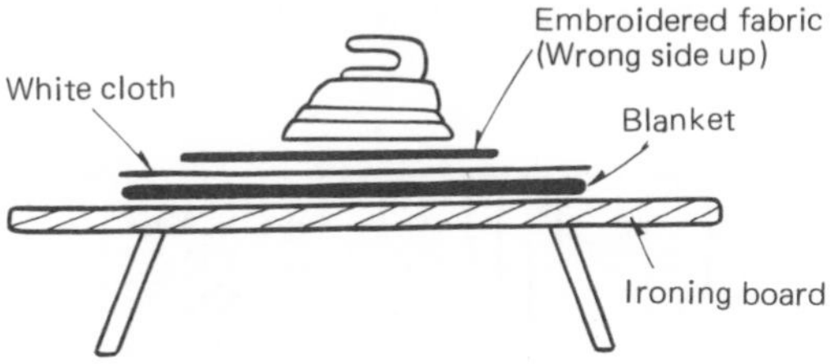

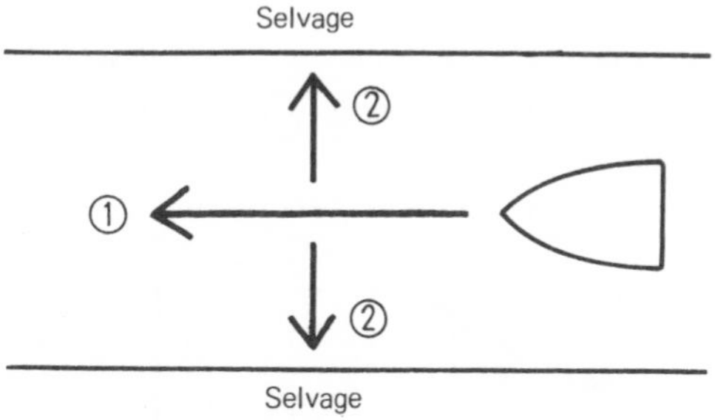

How to wash

It takes a long time to finish a piece of work and sometimes the fabric and the embroidery thread become soiled from working. If they are washable, wash gently with mild detergent and warm water. Rinse well, dry in the shade and press.

How to alter and make designs

How to enlarge or reduce designs

By using different thread count fabric . . . You can enlarge or reduce designs by using a fabric with different thread count. For example, the design worked on Indian cloth (50 threads per 4 inches) is smaller than that on Java canvas (35 threads per 4 inches).

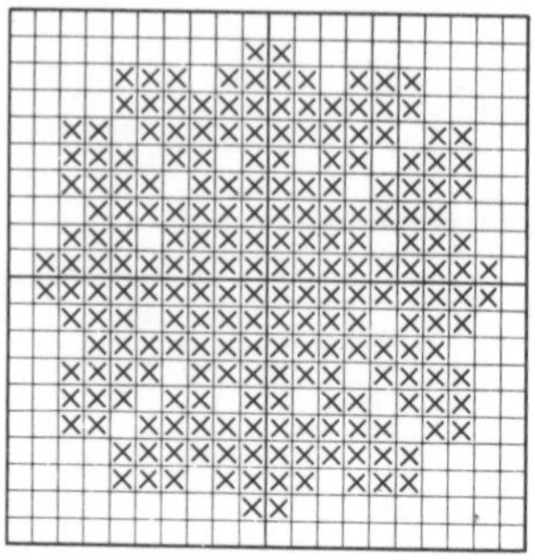

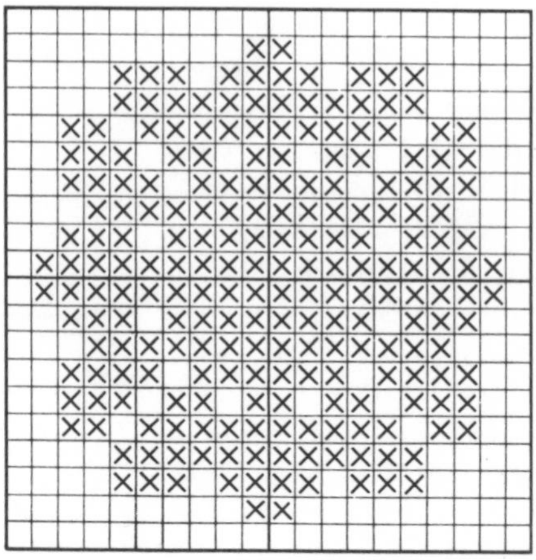

By multiplying the squares of the design . . . If the squares of the original design are doubled vertically and horizontally, the enlarged design has 4 by 4 squares. Besides, you can enlarge designs by working one cross over two or three fabric threads.

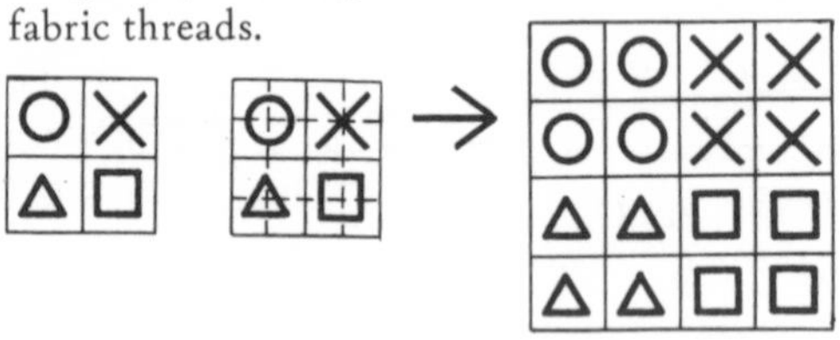

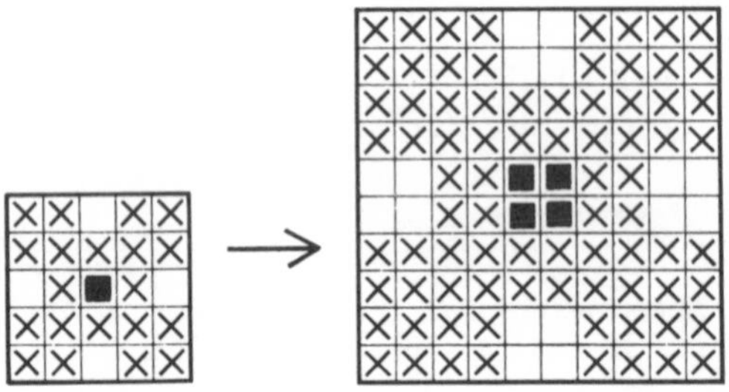

How to make designs for the Cross-Stitch Embroidery

If you want to work from your own design, make a sketch on a graph paper. Then fill the squares according to the original lines. Then color as you desire.

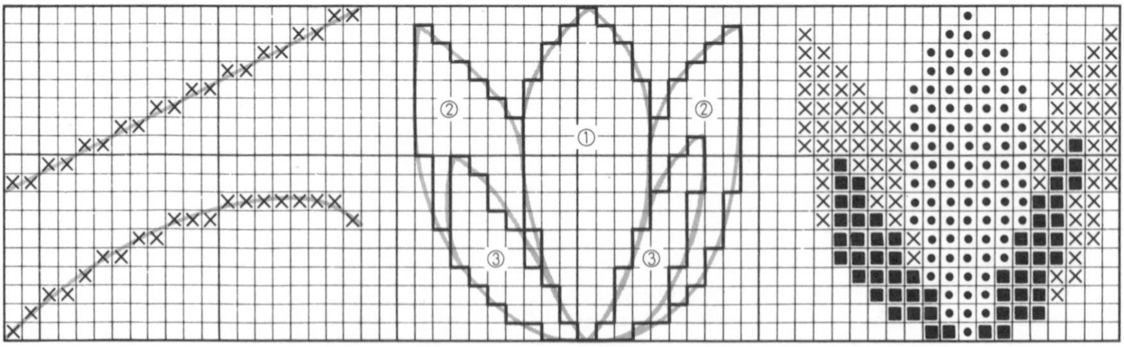

Color design as you desire.

How to work Cross-Stitch without using charts

The Cross-Stitch Embroidery is usually worked from charts, but you can work by following designs transfered on the fabric. First, transfer a design on the fabric using a dressmaker's carbon paper. Then, fill the design with cross-stitches. You can enlarge or reduce designs freely and also can use the same designs made for the Free-style Embroidery.